Step by Step Guide to
FLOWER ARRANGING

Barbara Pearce

Photography by Ken Lauder
Line drawings by Ian Garrard

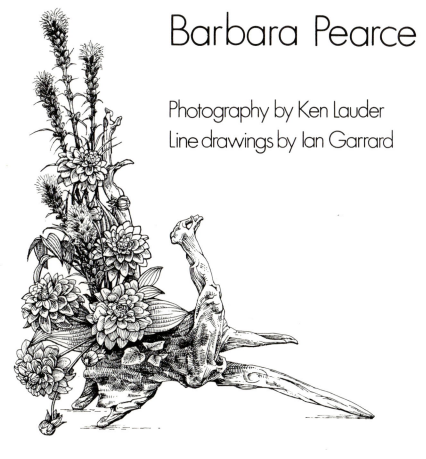

HAMLYN
London·New York·Sydney·Toronto

First published in 1973 by
The Hamlyn Publishing Group Limited
London · New York · Sydney · Toronto
Hamlyn House, Feltham, Middlesex, England

Filmset in Great Britain by
V. Siviter Smith & Co., Birmingham
Printed and bound in Great Britain by
Chapel River Press, Andover, Hampshire

Contents

PRACTICALITIES OF ARRANGING

Longer lasting flowers

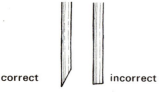

correct   incorrect

Treatment of soft stems

I hope that by the time you have read this book, you will have gained enough basic know-how and confidence to become a successful flower arranger. For simple reference I have divided the book into three parts. The first section deals with the preparation and choice of flowers and containers together with descriptions of the mechanics available, i.e. the tools and aids used to hold the plant material in the arrangement. In the second part I have explained how to do eight basic arrangements, detailing the guide lines you must learn in order to create attractive arrangements for yourself. In the last part there are many different examples of how you can adapt the basic arrangements to suit favourite containers, flowers and room settings.

Before attempting to arrange a collection of flowers and foliage, however, it is most important that you spend some time on giving the plant material the necessary treatment so that it will last longer in the finished arrangement. All flowers and foliage will benefit if they are given a long deep drink in a bucket which has been almost filled with tepid water. First, however, the ends of the stems must be treated so that they will take up water more readily. This preparation is necessary because, after flowers have been cut, the sap at the end of each stem dries quickly and forms a seal. It must be remembered that the following treatments should be carried out both when the flowers are given their initial drink and also, if you need to cut them again, when they are finally arranged and that they should be put into water immediately after they have been prepared.

Soft stems, for example daffodils, can usually take up water easily. Cut each stem on the slant—never straight across as there is then a danger that it will rest on the bottom of the bucket and will be unable to take up sufficient water. This cannot happen when the stem is cut at an angle as it then rests on the tip of the point. Such a cut will also give a larger area through which the stem can drink.

Woody stems, for example chrysanthemums, have greater difficulty in absorbing water. Make a slit up the centre of the end of each stem for about an inch. Alternatively, hammer the end of each stem so that the tissues are crushed. I find that hammering woody stems is quicker when preparing them for the initial drink but when cutting them to the required length for an arrangement, it is more convenient to slit them.

Preparation of woody stems

When hollow stems, like those of the lupin, are placed in water their tip ends always turn upwards which tends to spoil the final arrangement. To prevent this turn each flower upside down over the sink and with a small watering-can fill the stem with water. Do this very carefully to avoid air bubbles forming. Then you can either plug the stem with a small piece of Oasis or cotton wool and place it in the bucket of tepid water or simply hold your thumb over the bottom of the stem, put it into the water and take your thumb away. The pressure of the water in the bucket will keep the stem filled with water. When you cut the stem to the required length for the arrangement do this under water. If you need to cut a treated stem when it is out of water always turn it upside down. You can then cut it to the required length without losing any water.

Dahlias and young spring foliage will benefit from hot water treatment and it is also possible to revive flowers which droop after they have been in an arrangement for a day or two by dipping their ends into boiling water. This is particularly so with greenhouse-grown roses. Bring a pan of water to the boil and place the bottom inch of the stems into the water, having first protected the flower heads from the steam by wrapping them in either tissue paper or polythene bags. Leave them in the water for about twenty seconds and then take them out and place in tepid water which comes nearly up to their heads.

When some stems are cut, they give off a white milky substance and they are said to be 'bleeding'. Examples of flowers with this type of stem are members of the euphorbia family and poppies. Holding the ends of such stems in a match or gas flame for a few seconds will stop the bleeding. Again the petals must be protected.

All the hellebores including Christmas and Lenten roses, cyclamen flowers and polyanthus will last very much longer if their stems are slit up for about one inch on one side, starting an inch from the bottom.

Certain flowers and foliage—young spring foliage, artichoke leaves, violets and hydrangeas amongst them—last better if they are completely submerged while being given their initial drink. Violets take in a great deal of water through their petals and, even after submerging them for the first drink, it is advantageous to spray them overhead occasionally in the arrangement. If hydrangeas wilt after they have been arranged, they can be revived by placing the flower heads in water. They will take in water through their bracts and will quickly become refreshed.

And now for some general hints on the care of flowers and foliage. It is best to use warm water for the initial drink as flowers seem to accept this more readily and are refreshed quicker than when cold water is used. It is also important that flowers are not left out of water for too long as they wilt very quickly. The anémone is particularly bad in this respect.

Sometimes it is necessary to keep flowers for a time before they are arranged. If this is the case first treat them, put them in a bucket for their initial drink and then place this in a cool place, preferably on a stone floor. Roses can be rolled tightly in greaseproof paper to stop them opening too quickly.

Tulips, as I am sure most people have found out, are not the easiest flowers to arrange because their stems curve towards the light. The stems can be straightened by rolling them tightly, in the

Preparation of hollow stems

Hot water treatment

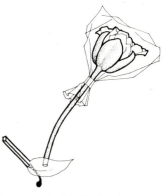

Treatment of 'bleeding' stems

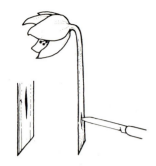

Preparation of a hellebore

Treatment by submersion

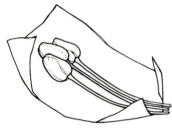

Preparation of tulips

same way as described for roses, and then placing them in deep water. Unfortunately, after a day in an arrangement, they will tend to revert to their old ways.

The water level in the container holding the arrangement should be looked at each day. On the first day it is advisable to look at it night and morning but afterwards once a day should be sufficient provided the room is not excessively hot. When topping up use tepid water as the water in the container can become fairly warm and it is rather a shock to the flowers if they are suddenly given cold water.

Before flowers and foliage are arranged, the leaves which will be submerged should be removed. If these leaves are left on, the water will quickly smell unpleasant but with clean stems it should stay comparatively fresh. It is not usually necessary to change the water once the flowers have been arranged but if clean water is needed, it should be tepid.

Some leaves and flowers have 'hairy' stems, for example *Begonia rex*, which can act as a syphon draining water out of the container to leave a pool of water on the furniture. To avoid this remove the hairs from that part of the stem which goes beneath the water by scraping it. Branches of lichen also need to have the ends of their stems cleaned for the same reason.

Before starting to arrange flowers and foliage, fill the container three-quarters full with water. Never fill to the rim at this stage because when the stems are placed into the container the water level will rise. When the arrangement is completed make sure the water is topped up to the rim.

The right container and accessory

The choice of containers and accessories is very important as they can either make or completely spoil an arrangement. Points to look out for are the suitability of the flowers and foliage to the container, the shape of the container in relation to the proposed shape of the arrangement, and the position of the finished arrangement in a room. First I shall describe the different shaped containers in detail and explain how and where each can be used.

CONTAINERS

Tazza : I find this elegant container the most useful of all. It is wide but shallow and is mounted on a stem which always gives an air of grace. The wider the top of the container the easier it is for arranging flowers and this is one of the reasons why I would always recommend a beginner to buy a tazza first.

It is very versatile, lending itself to many arrangements either for the centre of a table or for facing arrangements (symmetrical or asymmetrical) against a wall.

Bowls : Although not as elegant as the tazza, bowls are extremely useful. They look well in low all-round arrangements for the centre of a table. When used like this they are often known as posy bowls. They will also successfully accommodate facing arrangements (symmetrical or asymmetrical).

Large bowls are used in pedestal arrangements. A pastry mixing bowl, painted in a colour to match the pedestal, will do admirably. It is surprising how often kitchen bowls will double up for flower arranging to save the expense of buying a special container.

Urns: These are great favourites with flower arrangers. They are tall and usually fairly thin and as such are very graceful. They are more difficult to arrange because of their limited width and extra care needs to be taken when using them, as will be demonstrated later in the book. They are only suitable for facing arrangements (symmetrical or asymmetrical). All-round arrangements never look right in them because of the urn's relative height and width. This shape of vase looks attractive in a niche.

Oval: This shape, either as a flat oval dish or mounted on a stem, is probably most useful for a table centre and it looks especially lovely on an oval table. It will also hold facing arrangements (symmetrical, asymmetrical or L shaped) for a mantelpiece or similar position. When a symmetrical arrangement is created in an oval dish, it is better to keep it longer and lower than for a similar arrangement in either a tazza or urn.

Cylinder: This is a very popular shape as it looks well in modern homes. It is not the easiest shape to arrange because of the narrow opening at the top but when the right plant material is used, it can be most attractive. It is usually unsuitable for a traditional setting in a room furnished with antiques. However, in certain circumstances, and if you are very clever, the two can be blended together. An arrangement in a cylinder needs to be very tall and thin in keeping with the shape of the container.

Troughs: These are long and low and are used as table centres.

They are particularly good for long tables at formal dinners, or on mantelpieces, window-sills and shelves. They make excellent containers for church window-sills. A facing arrangement (symmetrical, asymmetrical or L shaped) in a trough can either be long and low or it can be quite tall, depending on the position in which it is placed. Wide troughs are particularly suitable for line arrangements. Troughs are made of various materials such as china, copper, brass, silver, pottery, wrought iron and basketwork.

Baskets: These can be found in a variety of shapes and when they are made out of basketwork they are especially suited to country-type flowers and informal arrangements. China and glass baskets are also available and these can contain more formal arrangements. Those fashioned out of basketwork will require water-tight linings and baking tins can be used successfully. These will need to be painted in order to seal them so use a colour to match the basketwork. It is best to have a matt finish paint rather than a gloss as this is less conspicuous. This inside container needs to be level with the rim of the basket and so it may need padding underneath.

Baskets with handles are extremely popular and there is a great range available both in size and shape, including the trug basket. This is more difficult to use than most because of the low handle which must, of course, be seen after the flowers have been arranged.

Very pretty arrangements can be created in baskets with lids but these containers are not quite so useful as those with handles as they are unsuitable for all-round arrangements. Never cover all the lid with flowers and foliage.

Shells: Containers fashioned in the shape of a shell are pretty for flower arrangements. Try, however, to keep the shape of the shell which usually results in a long, low arrangement.

Adaptable containers: Some containers can be used which were not originally meant to hold flowers. Many Victorian *objet d'arts* can be converted. Needlework, writing and Bible boxes have great potential and can become favourites for flower arrangements. They will need water-holding linings and painted baking tins are again ideal. The lids of such boxes make good backgrounds to the flowers and they can be very attractively lined with material. Pieces of wood cut to fit inside the lid can be covered with different coloured and textured materials attached by Sellotape. In this way a range can be built up so that you will have the appropriate colour and also texture of material to go with whatever flowers and foliage you want to use. Make sure that the material looks right with the particular wood of the box. For shiny woods satin or velvet look well. Only facing arrangements can be done in these boxes and an L shape is ideal.

Victorian oil lamps can also be used from time to time by making a simple conversion. Remove the wick and replace it with a candle-cup. Glass oil lamps look beautiful with matching flowers but lamps can also be found in china, silver and gilt. Arrangements can be all round or facing but if the lamp is very tall it will look better with a facing arrangement.

Silver meat covers make splendid flower containers if they are inverted on a stand. You may be able to persuade a blacksmith to make a wrought-iron stand for one and if you are going to make a lot of use of such a container have two stands made—a low one for table centres and a taller stand for facing arrangements (symmetrical or asymmetrical).

Very inexpensive containers can be made from the wicker pads in which spring flowers arrive from France. These are quite large so they will hold a lot of flowers. A baking-tin lining will be needed and they will then be ideal for the types of arrangements suitable for boxes.

Vegetable dishes and frying pans make original containers. Brass frying pans are particularly good especially when arranged with red or orange flowers. With a little imagination a wealth of containers will be found in the kitchen. A meat plate with a small water-holding container made out of an empty salmon tin would make an excellent container for a line arrangement.

Dual-purpose containers: I have already mentioned the various types of containers such as the tazza which can be used for more than one type of arrangement. If you do not want to buy many containers or if you have limited storage space, the following are the best: tazza, bowl, trough, and basket with a handle.

ACCESSORIES

Flower scissors: Specially designed flower scissors are available and are essential equipment for the arranger. They incorporate two useful features—a serrated edge which is useful for cutting heavy stems and a wire-cutting groove.

Candlecups: These are small containers which are designed to fit on to candlesticks. They are available in various sizes and they can also be fitted into the necks of bottles which make appropriate flower containers for parties. Candlecups are made in chrome, brass, copper, and white or coloured plastic and are inexpensive. Although they can be used for facing arrangements, they are better suited to all-round ones. If you have a three-branched candelabra around which you would like to create an arrangement, either fit a candlecup on each side and leave the centre free, or have one candlecup in the centre and leave the two sides free. When using a candlecup for an all-round arrangement, especially at Christmas, try to include a candle in the centre.

Cones or tubes: Although these are seldom needed for arrangements in the home, they are excellent when creating pedestal arrangements in churches or for receptions. They are used to give extra length to stems when it is impossible to obtain flowers with long enough stems to achieve the correct proportions in large arrangements.

First attach the cone to a green-painted square stick with Sellotape so that cone and stick overlap by about three inches. A square stick is better than a round one because a round one will tend to twist in the netting, whereas a square one will hold its position. The length of the stick depends on the height of the arrangement and the length of the flower stems. For a pedestal arrangement three cones are usually sufficient but in a really vast arrangement as many as twenty could be used. This, however, is exceptional. More explanation on their use will be found in the description of a pedestal arrangement on page 57.

Blocks of glass: These are useful to place at the base of the container in a line arrangement to cover the pinholder. Position them so that they run through beneath the flowers and foliage. The glass will look like ice and give an illusion of coolness and so it is particularly lovely in summer arrangements. Colourless glass is

A cone attached to a square stick by Sellotape

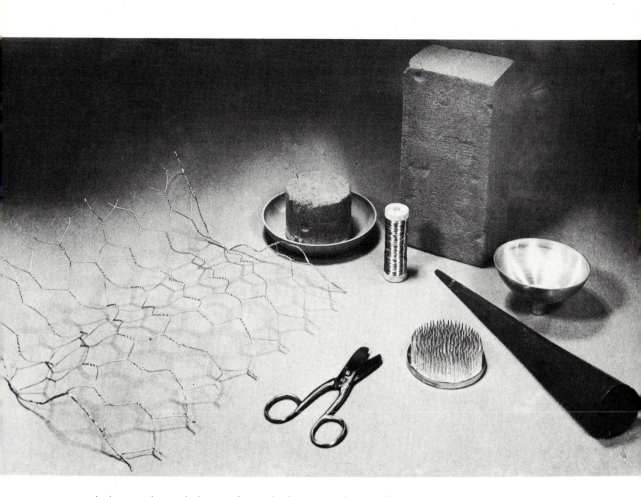

more natural than coloured, but coloured glass can be used to match up with a particular flower. Take care, however, as some flowers like the chrysanthemum never look very happy with glass arranged beneath them. If you are unable to obtain small pieces of glass they can be made by using glass from shattered windscreens which you may be able to get at your local garage. Cover a pebble with silver paper. Paste this over with a strong clear glue and then completely cover the pebble with two layers of the shattered windscreen. Shattered windscreen may also be used on its own.

Pebbles: These can be used in a similar way to glass. I have collected many different ones from river banks, especially those in Scotland and Wales, and the seashore. Their colours can be beautiful—white, pink, grey, brown and mauve. Some have metallic streaks in them and it is usually possible to find a pebble which echoes the colour of a particular flower. They are preferable to glass in the more unsophisticated or country type of arrangement which uses daffodils, dahlias and others. They are also more at home in the heavier pottery containers.

Both pepples and glass should be placed so that they present a casual appearance. They do, however, need careful positioning so that they enhance the design of an arrangement and do not spoil the effect.

Shells: These can be used in arrangements of seashore flowers such as sea holly (eryngium). Coral also makes an interesting accessory.

Driftwood : This is very much sought after by the flower arranger and it can be very difficult to find a piece with a really good shape. Although driftwood can be bought, often it has been bleached and I prefer it in the natural state—you will certainly value it more if you are lucky enough to find a piece for yourself. Beaches and the shores of lochs and lakes are the more likely hunting grounds. If it is the right shape, driftwood can form part of the actual container for the flowers but generally it is used as an accessory and is particularly effective in simple arrangements using just a few varieties or, better still, one kind of flower.

Figurines : These are mainly used as accessories in competitive flower arranging in helping to interpret a theme like a song or book title. They should always be less important than the flowers and foliage. I prefer to keep an arrangement natural and not to incorporate figurines but some people have a favourite one which they like to use.

Candles : These make effective and useful accessories, especially when creating an arrangement in a candlecup. They are also attractive in the centre of long and low arrangements where they can give height. A candle holder is placed in the centre of such an arrangement to hold the candle. This has spikes in its base which will hold it on to Oasis or a pinholder.

How to hold flowers in their containers

In this chapter I shall describe the various methods used to hold plant material in position in an arrangement. Everyone has their favourite aid and as each new one comes on to the market, it is tried and tested and usually the flower arranger finds that it has a particular part to play. I must admit, however, that I still prefer the old method of wire netting for the majority of arrangements.

Wire netting : I use a mesh of 2 in. and to me this is preferable to the smaller size which is available. It can be rolled tighter if needed for thinner stems and there is more space to take larger stems without damaging them.

You will find by means of trial and error how much netting is required for a container. This varies with the type of flower to be used and the thickness of the stems. On the whole the stems of spring flowers are thicker than those produced during the rest of the year so less netting will therefore be needed for these.

The wire netting must be firmly secured in the container otherwise you are unlikely to achieve a successful arrangement. First select the size of netting required, then consider the depth and width of the container. It is impossible to give exact measurements of the piece of netting needed for a certain container as some people like a little more and others less. As a rough guide, however, a medium-sized bowl needs about $\frac{1}{2}$ to $\frac{3}{4}$ yd. of 18 in. high, 2-in. mesh. It is much better to have one large piece of netting. If you only have two smaller pieces then it is advisable to join them together by twisting the edge of one around the other.

Next loosely roll the netting from one corner to the other so that you end up with four or five layers. After it has been rolled in this

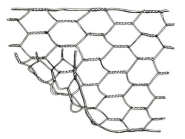

Wire netting is rolled from one corner to the diagonally opposite corner

way consider the shape of the container to be used. With a bowl or tazza, the two ends need to be bent right into the centre and the netting gently forced into a rounded shape. With an urn, keep the netting narrow at the bottom then push it into the container. When a trough is being used bend the ends of the netting in a little way. Some of the netting should always touch the bottom of the container and it should be level with the rim and slightly raised in the centre where the longer stems are placed. Spread the netting evenly out in the container.

The next step is to secure the netting and this can be done in two ways. If the container has a lip, some of the edges of the netting can be clipped over this. Five or six strands fastened at equal distances are sufficient to hold the netting firmly and they will be hidden once the arrangement is completed. If there is no suitable lip then the netting will have to be tied into the container. Thirty-gauge silver wire, which can be purchased on a reel and is similar to fuse wire, is the best for this purpose. If silver wire is not available then a fairly fine string can be substituted. Tie the wire or string around the container as if you were tying up a parcel and finish by knotting firmly at the top of the netting. If the container has a stem then take the wire around this once or twice and then tie it both ways over the bowl. If, after the arrangement is completed, the wire or string is noticeable, it can be cut away and the flowers should remain in position. If you are using a china container then the netting could be secured with Sellotape. However, never do this with valuable containers as it can mark them. This is especially so with silver, copper, brass, pewter and other metalware.

It is not necessary to remove the netting each time an arrange-

Wire netting is rolled into four or five layers

Wire netting shaped to fit a tazza

13

ment is dismantled. Rinse the container thoroughly under the tap before putting it away and occasionally take out the netting and give the vase a good scrub.

Water-retaining substances: There are several on the market with probably the best known being Oasis. This needs to be thoroughly soaked so that when the stems of the flowers are anchored into it, they do not meet any dry patches.

Oasis can be cut to the required shape whether it is wet or dry. It can be used on its own in a goblet-type or any small container but when it is used in a larger vase with bigger flowers then a small piece of netting placed over the Oasis and tied into position is an advantage. Unfortunately, Oasis is more costly than wire netting because it cannot be used indefinitely. After it has been used for three or four arrangements it crumbles and will not hold the stems firmly.

Never fill a container completely with Oasis as it will then be impossible to give the arrangement fresh water. This must be done as the flowers drink water from Oasis at the same rate as a conventional arrangement using wire netting and the water level must be checked regularly in the same way.

Oasis is difficult to use with soft-stemmed flowers but stiff-stemmed flowers will be anchored quite firmly. With daffodils or similar-stemmed flowers, you may have to make a hole in the Oasis first with a pencil and then put the flower stem into this.

Oasis holders: These are useful when Oasis is used on its own. Although similar to a pinholder (see later), they only have about six spikes which are each about $1\frac{1}{4}$ in. high. The Oasis is placed on to these spikes and is held firmly by them. They are useful when using heavier branches because the extra weight at the base helps to balance the branch.

Oasis cradles: These can be made when glass containers are being used. Although it is quite in order to see the stems of the flowers through the glass, you should not be able to see the mechanics. Take a small piece of wire netting and push the centre about two inches down inside the container and clip the edges around the rim. When this netting is firmly in position, put in the soaked Oasis so that it comes just above the rim of the glass container. Three-quarters fill this with water. The stems of the flowers and foliage are then pushed into the Oasis. The tallest ones at the back can go straight down into the container. The flowers which come out over the edge should be placed horizontally into the Oasis. Make sure that the leaves and flowers over the edge cover the Oasis cradle as this should not be seen when the arrangement is completed.

The fitment of an Oasis cradle

Pinholders: These are one of the most useful aids to flower arrangement and they are available in different sizes. They are used underneath wire netting in shallow containers to hold the heavier stems at the back of an arrangement. This can save much time and patience as it will prevent the longer-stemmed flowers moving. Oasis can be used in a similar way.

Another use for the pinholder is in a line arrangement on a flat dish. A heavy pinholder is needed, preferably one which is lead based so that it holds the flowers without toppling. It may be necessary to stick the pinholder to the container with Bostik Blu-tack or a similar harmless product but I would advise against this if at all possible as some adhesives may spoil the surface of the container. If the flowers are balanced correctly there is no likelihood of them falling over. It is certainly worth paying extra for a heavier pinholder. You can buy pinholders with the spikes close together or further apart. For heavier-stemmed flowers and foliage you will need the spikes further apart.

Gravel: Sometimes when large heavy flowers are used in a container which is relatively light, the arrangement can become unstable and topple. This should not happen if the finished arrangement is correctly balanced but you might run into difficulties when making it up. Gravel or even sand can be placed in the bottom of the container to make it heavier. The gravel will not harm the flowers and will not take up too much room in the container.

Pedestals: When using flat, relatively light bowls on pedestals, these should be attached to their stands with string or thick wire to hold them firmly in position. When the container is heavier and urn shaped this is not necessary. With a pedestal arrangement in a marquee, it is advisable to anchor it well as the ground is more uneven and it could topple. If a wrought-iron pedestal is to be used, this can be staked to the ground.

Narrow-necked containers: These include the narrow-necked altar vases which are found in many churches. They are extremely difficult to arrange because there is only room for perhaps two or three stems in their necks. To overcome this secure a candlecup in the neck with silver wire. Alternatively a funnel, which has been plugged with a cork to stop the water running through, can be used in the same way.

A candlecup fitted into a narrow-necked vase

Colour schemes in flower arrangement

Colour plays a very large part in successful flower arranging. If an arrangement has a good colour balance but is lacking in other respects it will still be attractive and receive attention. The appreciation of colour is a very personal thing and I am purposely not going to be over technical as I believe that good colour sense will come with experience. Here, however, are some colour schemes and ideas to help you.

Monochromatic: This is a colour scheme which uses the tints and shades of one particular colour or hue and it can be very attractive. The tint is the hue with white added and the shade the hue with black added. Extreme care must be taken to make sure that the colours are correct. For example with pink flowers you will need to use either the blue pinks or the yellow pinks as mixing the two will not give the blending of colours necessary for this scheme. You will soon acquire a flair for this, however, although it is not always easy to obtain just the colour of flower which you may require to do this kind of arrangement. It is impossible for a florist to carry a full range of all the colours.

Clashing colours: This scheme uses the clashing colours contained inside one hue and it can be great fun. For a red arrangement you will need the blue reds and also the yellow reds, going from magenta to a bright orange. It is surprising how attractive this can look, especially on a dinner table where it will provide a good talking point, but you must place such an arrangement with care in a room setting. Red probably lends itself better to this colour scheme than any other hue but pink can also be used successfully in this way.

Analogous: To explain an analogous colour scheme you really need to picture in your mind a colour wheel. First think of the colours of the rainbow—red, orange, yellow, green, blue, indigo, violet—and then form them into a wheel by putting the red next to the violet. To take this a step further, imagine this central circle flanked by an outer circle of the same colours with white added giving the tints and an inner circle with black added to give the shades. In this way an arrangement can be built up on a red, red-orange and orange scheme or a yellow—green, green and blue-green theme and so on. This is a very useful type of colour scheme especially when it is impossible to obtain shades and tints of one colour. When using this type of scheme try to use the lightest of the colours at the top of the arrangement and also on the widest points as they will show up so much better.

Mixed colours: Many people like to see mixed colours in an arrangement and this can be achieved in one of four different ways. The first is known as a Dutch group and this borrows the colours from a Dutch flower painting. The second way is with mixed garden flowers. The third uses the Victorian idea of colour and the fourth pastel shades.

The Dutch flower paintings are remarkable for their colourful arrangements of flowers from different seasons. Tulips, often striped ones, fritillaries, pheasant eye narcissi, poppies, open roses and many others are seen together. It is fun to study the colours and types of flowers in these paintings although it is not necessary to copy them exactly but simply to follow along the same lines and to make your arrangements as mixed as possible.

For an arrangement of garden flowers go into the garden and collect one or two of each kind and colour of flower. It is best to leave out the white flowers because the eye immediately goes to these and is detracted from the rest. If you do use white place it near the centre of the arrangement. Lime-green flowers are very good in a mixed arrangement. They blend in well and lend a sharpness to the composition. There is a surprisingly wide selection of green flowers such as *Alchemilla mollis*, *Amaranthus viridis*, lime-green nicotiana, the green zinnia called Envy and many of the euphorbias. Yellow flowers bring out the colours of others, so try to include them. It is better to choose different shaped flowers which will give added interest.

The Victorian idea of colour was rather hard and they used bright and gaudy hues. Try to use the flowers which would have been available then such as geraniums and pack them in tightly or place them in an epergne or a piece of Victorian glass to complete the effect. These Victorian arrangements will, of course, look especially attractive in rooms furnished with antiques.

Pastel colours are especially effective when used in small spring arrangements of flowers such as pale pink roman hyacinths, primroses, blue muscari, pale green hellebores and mauve freesia. They are also useful for a children's party decoration and one pretty idea which should delight a small girl is to lead trails of ribbon from an arrangement to each child's place at the table with a present on the end. Pastel-coloured flowers look well when arranged in a natural way by having clumps of flowers on a dish with bun moss. The dark green of the moss sets off the pastel shades.

Complementary: These are the colours which are opposite to each other in the colour wheel and an arrangement using them is most successful when they are of equal intensity, for example clear red with clear green or apricot with cobalt blue.

Arrangements of one colour with white: Pastel colours are the best to use with white because they do not provide such a contrast. Red and white should not be seen together for this reason, apart from the fact that many people are superstitious about using these colours.

Foliage colour: With any colour scheme of flowers, it is usually possible to obtain foliage which complements it. For example red flowers blend well with reddish foliage or red-stemmed foliage; pink and blue flowers look well with grey foliage; orange flowers with leaves tinted and shaded orange. Yellow flowers are especially good with yellow and lime-green foliage, and white flowers also look attractive with lime-green leaves. The foliage belonging to the flowers being arranged is always suitable and it is, of course, more natural but if the foliage colour does match the flowers it adds that extra something.

Coloured containers: These can cause problems because of matching the flowers to them. The most useful colour is dull yellow-green as many different coloured flowers will look well against it. White containers can be rather obvious and create too great a contrast to the colour of the flowers. Orange and other brightly coloured containers are useful for some colours but can be limiting.

Silver and pewter containers are particularly good arranged with whites, pinks, mauves and, especially at Christmas time, reds. Copper is ideal for red and orange flowers and for mixed green flowers and foliage. Brass is excellent with yellow flowers and again a mixed green colouring. Basketwork is better with orange, red, mixed colouring and yellow.

The colour scheme of the setting: An arrangement should never look too obvious in a room. It should blend in with the furnishing and become part of the surroundings. This does not mean that you need to use the same colour scheme and flowers every time. When a room is designed around two colours you can emphasise one of these colours one week and the other the next. The third week the two colours could be blended together. You need not use the exact colour of the room but a tint or shade of the colour. This will again give interest. You can also vary the containers so that the shape of the arrangement will change too. Use mixed flowers of the chosen colour or just one kind of flower and change the position of the arrangement in the room.

If a room has been furnished in neutral colours then an arrangement to brighten it will be attractive. A Dutch group could be used in this case. If there is a painting on the wall, compose an arrangement using flowers in the same colouring. A mirror is a useful feature because by creating an arrangement of mixed greens to reflect into it, an impression of coolness can be achieved and this can be effective especially in hot weather.

When sending a gift of flowers try to remember the colouring of the room they will be going in. If this is not known keep to neutral colours like cream.

It is important to take into account the light intensity of the room. Blue, for example, is a very poor colour if the room is fairly dark, especially if it is being used with lighter coloured flowers such as white. In any case never use blue at the top of an arrangement with white flowers immediately beneath. The blue flowers will disappear leaving the white standing out well and this will make the arrangement an odd shape. Any colour which has blue in it will not show up well in a dark room and this includes the blue pinks, blue reds and purples. Yellow flowers and colours with yellow in them will show up very well from a distance, whereas the blues will not. Keep blue for daylight rather than artificial light.

Special occasion flowers and their colours: Good flowers will make an occasion even more special. Send golden-yellow flowers for a golden wedding anniversary; use pink flowers for a girl's christening. These colours may be very traditional but I think people still prefer to keep to them. For a girl's twenty-first or eighteenth birthday link the colours of the flowers with the colouring in her dress. For a wedding I think the church flowers and also those for the reception should echo the dresses of either the bride or the bridesmaids. In the church the white or cream of the bride's dress are best as these will show up well in the darkness of the church.

If you regularly arrange flowers for the church, you will know that certain festivals need special flowers and colours. I especially like the lightness of daffodils with primroses at Easter.

Choosing your plant material

The choice of flowers and foliage to be used is of the utmost importance in flower arranging especially as the interest is partly derived from this aspect.

Flower types: For the purposes of arranging, flowers can be classed into three groups. First there are the pointed flowers. These have many flowers borne closely on each stem. The pointed effect is produced because the flowers gradually open in succession starting with the lowest. Those at the top are only in bud form when the flowers at the bottom are at their best and so the spike gradually tapers to a point. Examples include gladioli, delphiniums, larkspur and stocks.

The second group also have many flowers to each stem but each of them is borne on a separate secondary stalk to give a bunchy appearance. Examples include spray chrysanthemums with flowers originating from all down the stem and alstroemerias with the flowers deriving from one point at the top of the stem.

The third class comprises the flowers which are carried singly at the end of one main stem. These flowers have a variety of shapes. There are both single and double kinds, those with flat faces and those with trumpets. Examples include daffodils and many members of the daisy family.

When creating an arrangement of mixed flowers, it is better to combine these various shapes. Pointed flowers will make good

Delphinium—a pointed flower

main outline flowers to an arrangement as they will provide an air of lightness. Do not use bunchy flowers high on the periphery of an arrangement unless you are able to use even larger material lower in the outline as this will look top heavy and you will ruin the effect. Ideally it is better to use two kinds of pointed flower.

The value of grouping will, I hope, become clear to you when you start to do some of the basic arrangements. For example the basic facing arrangement in a tazza incorporates five different kinds of flowers. There are two pointed ones, larkspur and campanula, and two round ones, roses and carnations. The peonies are large and heavy and these give weight and interest to the arrangement in the centre. The larkspur are grouped with the roses and these are positioned through the arrangement from high on the right to low on the left with the campanula and carnations going the opposite way. This grouping gives a more even distribution of weight and therefore good balance. Smaller flowers should always be used on the outline edge and higher throughout an arrangement with the larger flowers nearer the centre and lower.

If you combine single and bunchy flowers in an arrangement, you will find that you will need more single flowers to balance the multi-headed ones. When using only single flowers try to get as much variation of shape as possible.

Foliage types: The choice of foliage needs the same consideration. Single leaves have various shapes. They can be broad and rounded like the bergenia; oval and pointed like hosta; heart shaped like the leaf of the arum lily; irregular like *Begonia rex* or have a serrated edge like the artichoke. These leaves are used to give heart to an arrangement especially when light spiky flowers are incorporated. Their weight will help to hold an arrangement together and to give it solidity. Even when doing a small arrangement you can still use larger leaves in the centre though, of course, these must be in scale with the rest of the plant material. Ideal in these circumstances are ivy and scindapsis. An uneven number of leaves are used in the centre but it would be very unusual to need more than nine. These leaves should not be overcrowded as this would defeat the object of keeping a clean cut centre. You can also use whole rosettes of leaves in the centre of an arrangement instead of large, single leaves. House plants, for example aspidistras and caladiums, can be a very attractive source of such material.

For our purposes compound leaves can be described as those with many leaves to a stem and these can be grouped with the flowers through an arrangement. It is better to have two kinds of this type of foliage in an arrangement so that one kind can be arranged with one group and the other with the second. Examples include pittosporum and box with the individual leaves quite small and Portuguese laurel and gaultheria which are quite large. When choosing the foliage to go with certain flowers try to get a good contrast to provide interest and balance. If the flowers are fussy, select a clean cut foliage like gaultheria. If, however, the flowers are single, a more fussy foliage like pittosporum could be used.

Lastly, there are the tall thin leaves of the reed type. Since these grow naturally upright, they should be positioned reasonably vertically in an arrangement. This type of leaf is valuable for estab-

Spray chrysanthemum—a bunchy flower

Daffodil—a single flower

Bergenia—a single leaf

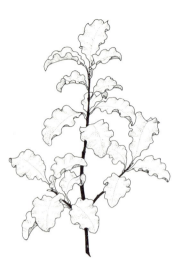

Pittosporum—a compound leaf

Reed—a tall thin leaf

lishing the height of an arrangement. Never make a fan of them as this looks particularly ugly.

Ferns: These can be used upright in an arrangement or sideways along the edge as both ways will emulate their natural habit.

Grasses: These will add lightness and interest to an arrangement. Many seedsmen offer a wide variety of ornamental grasses from which you can make a selection if you want to try growing some of the many different forms in your own garden. As with the reed type of leaf always arrange grasses upright.

Twigs and branches: These are very useful for giving shape to a line arrangement and for providing interest in a mass arrangement. My favourites are the alder and stripped lime together with those which are covered in lichen. I am also very fond of the following subjects which flower early in the spring before the foliage appears—*Hamamelis mollis*, *Chimonanthus fragrans*, daphnes, willows and hazels.

Lichen-covered branches are found in the damp areas on the west side of Great Britain. Lichen is formed by the symbiotic association of a fungus and an alga i.e. a fungus and an alga existing together for their common good. It is often found on fir trees but if you can find it on less brittle wood then these pieces can be stored for several years without disintegrating. When arranging lichen-covered branches that portion which is to go under water should be scraped free of lichen as this will syphon water out of the container.

Alder trees are generally found beside rivers, ponds, lakes and other damp habitats and the twigs are attractive in winter and spring with their small cones and catkins. The catkins do not produce their pollen until the spring but they are still excellent for winter decoration.

The bracts of the lime tree develop in high summer though these might not be readily noticed when the tree is in full leaf. If you are lucky enough to have access to a tree you can judiciously cut off some of the elegant stems. Trim away the leaves to reveal the lime-green bracts. You could use the stripped lime so prepared in both mass and line arrangements.

Stripped lime can be preserved with glycerine and it can then be kept for several months. To do this slit the ends of the stems and give them a short drink. Then place the bottoms of the stems into a solution of two parts glycerine to one part hot water. Leave them for a week to ten days until the lime has turned an attractive brown colour.

Hazelnut catkins are firm favourites with flower arrangers and most attractive when used with daffodils. Other catkin-bearing subjects include the willow and one species has the additional interest of contorted branches. Pleasing arrangements can be achieved with just a few catkin branches and a group of large leaves beneath to cover the pinholder. The pretty branches of daphne are beautiful in association with just a few flowers which pick up the colour of the daphne. *Hamamelis mollis* is another good early-flowering shrub, as is *Chimonanthus fragrans*.

Many other beautiful woody subjects can be found in garden and countryside. It is important, however, when you are cutting twigs from a shrub or tree that you do this very carefully so that you do not spoil its overall shape.

Bulrushes: These give the flower arranger another interesting

20

shape. They should be used upright and several of differing lengths placed at the top of an arrangement working down towards the centre will prove very attractive. I think that the natural-coloured ones are much to be preferred to the dyed ones.

Berries and seedheads: These are invaluable for autumn arrangements. They can be used on their own with just a little foliage or combined with both flowers and foliage. There are many attractive berries available in a wide range of colours. It is, therefore, quite easy to match a particular flower with a berry. Heavier sprays of berries are best kept to the centre of an arrangement but lighter branches can be grouped throughout. If necessary, clip some of the leaves off the branches to show the berries more clearly but do not completely defoliate them..

When using seedheads with just a small amount of foliage, try to have as many different shapes as possible. Examples include clematis, both cultivated and wild, delphiniums, lupins, poppies, honesty, philadelphus, buddleia and teasels.

Availability of plant material: You may not be able to find some of the flowers which I have used in the arrangements in this book and I hope that this will not deter you for there are many other similar flowers which can be substituted. Some of you will not have a garden but a wealth of material can be gathered from the hedgerow and many of the flowers can be bought from the florist. If you only have a small garden and would like to cultivate some material for arranging, I would strongly recommend you to grow foliage rather than flowers. It is far easier to buy flowers than foliage—at least, interesting foliage. You can even grow a few ivies, which are most useful for flower arrangement, in a window-box.

How many flowers? It is very difficult for a beginner to determine how many flowers are needed for a mass arrangement. This depends on the size of the container, where the arrangement is to be placed and the size of the flowers. It is not easy for me to give you much guidance in this respect but as an example a medium-sized urn with a facing arrangement would need roughly three-and-a-half dozen flowers. The right judgement will come with experience and when you become accustomed to your containers. You will then be able to tell by eye the number of flowers you will need when picking from the garden or buying from a florist.

Never overcrowd an arrangement; each flower needs space around it. It is always better to have too few rather than too many flowers. Remember, too, that a bud will open into a flower and always leave sufficient space so that when it does open it will not smother its neighbours.

The amount of foliage used is fairly critical. A massed arrangement with fewer flowers will need more foliage. When using leaves as fillers to the flowers do not put in too many as a forest effect can quickly be achieved. Foliage will look most untidy unless it is used with care.

If you are to have less than a dozen flowers in an arrangement keep to an uneven number. The tendency is to arrange an even number in pairs which will result in a very regimented effect. With an uneven number this is unlikely. Also have an uneven number of leaves.

Flowers with their own foliage: It will look more natural if the foliage of the flowers to be arranged can also be used, in which case it must be grouped through the arrangement with the flower to which it belongs. Leave the compound leaves of roses attached to a piece of the main stem. This will help when securing them into an arrangement. Tulip leaves are sometimes rather large and heavy. To overcome this, they can be cut short and the cut ends rolled round pieces of stem which will help to hold them into the netting. Daffodil leaves are very attractive when used with their flowers. Bunches of three or five are more effective especially if each leaf in the bunch is placed at a different length. They should never be longer than the flowers.

Dahlia foliage is good but it should receive hot water treatment before being arranged. Peonies, too, have long lasting leaves. These should be cut leaving a piece of main stem attached as for roses. These are just a few examples of leaves which can be used with their own flowers.

The right flower for the container: Another aspect to consider is the suitability of flowers to the container. Daffodils, a country-type flower, do not look right arranged in a sophisticated glass container. They look their best in basketwork, brass, copper, heavy-type pottery and cork bark. Roses can be arranged in a variety of containers. Florist's roses look quite well in glass or porcelain. The more robust-looking garden roses of yellow, orange and red shades look very happy in basketwork. Arum lilies are most attractive arranged with their own foliage on a flat glass or china dish so that the water can be seen around them. Chrysanthemums are quite adaptable to containers and they look well in basketwork, copper, brass, pottery and silver. A mixture of summer flowers is lovely in a basket. In fact all garden-type flowers are attractive in basketwork containers. The more sophisticated flowers look well in silver, glass and porcelain.

Here is a suggested list of what colour and texture of container would most readily suit a particular coloured flower. *Red flowers*—copper; wooden boxes; black pottery; basketwork; pewter. *Orange flowers*—copper; stone; basketwork; gilt. *White flowers*—white china; silver; gilt; mirror; plain, blue or green glass. *Pink flowers*—silver; pewter; plain, pink or green glass; green, white, grey or pink china. *Blue flowers*—grey, green or white china; silver; plain, blue or green glass; mirror. *Yellow flowers*—green or white china; brass; wooden boxes; basketwork; gilt. *Green flowers*—green pottery; brass; mirror; glass. *Mauve flowers*—grey or white china; silver; pewter; mirror; glass. With a combination of colours choose a container suitable for all of them.

Large arrangements: The flowers and leaves for large arrangements need to be on a much bigger scale than arrangements for the home. Big bold flowers will always look more effective as these arrangements are usually seen from a distance. It is still necessary to incorporate the different shapes of flowers and foliage and there are a host of large flowers and leaves which could be used.

Flowers to suit the style of the setting: Try to use flowers which blend in with the room setting. For example an ultra-modern room needs modern line arrangements with just a few flowers to match the colour of the room. A Victorian room should have an arrangement in a Victorian container. The elegant room should have an arrangement in a tazza or urn and for a country cottage a basket of mixed garden flowers is the most attractive.

EIGHT BASIC ARRANGEMENTS

Introduction

This section contains detailed descriptions of eight basic arrangements explained in an instructional manner. To avoid repeating myself I have assumed that for each arrangement you will choose and prepare your plant material and container as advised in the first section of this book.

You will not have the exact containers as those shown in the photographs but as long as they are of a similar shape and care is taken in selecting the flowers and foliage to go in them you will be successful. I am sure that if you use different materials when creating the arrangements which follow you will find it more challenging and far more rewarding when they are a success.

I have summarised below the main principles which should be applied when creating successful arrangements as a rough guide to help you remember and these points are explained more fully in the arrangements which follow.

1. Grouping is perhaps the most important factor in obtaining a balanced effect. Remember when choosing your flowers to select a good variation in shape, together with an attractive colour balance.

2. Good variation of stem length throughout an arrangement is also necessary. Never have two flowers of the same length side by side.

3. Keep the larger flowers lower in the arrangement and the smaller ones of each kind on the outline and throughout the arrangement to give a light touch.

4. All the stems should appear to radiate from the tallest in the arrangement.

5. Never have crossing stems in an arrangement.

6. Always position a stem so that the flower head is exactly where it is required. Never try to move a flower head after the stem has been secured.

7. Leave plenty of space around each subject in an arrangement especially buds which will open and expand. Do not overcrowd the flowers.

8. Try to keep the arrangement as natural as possible. This depends to a large extent on the shape and curvature of the stems to be used. The flowers should never be rigid and they will look more natural if some of them are placed so that they are facing to the side rather than looking straight ahead, especially if they are flowers with an 'eye' i.e. a single flower with a flat face.

9. When using mixed flowers, it is better to have at least three different kinds of flower but two would be permissible.

10. A broken line around the edge of an arrangement is very important. This is created by having the flowers in the outline at different lengths so that they give an uneven impression and not a trimmed look.

11. Never make the main flowers in the centre of an arrangement look too obvious. Other plant material, which is lighter in weight and longer stemmed, should be arranged through the centre.

12. When creating a facing arrangement always remember to fill in at the back to hide the netting and give a finished appearance.

13. Arrangements should never look flat when they are seen from the side. By building out from the tallest flower at the back to the longest over the front edge with lighter weight flowers you should be able to achieve a triangular effect from this angle too. The line drawings showing the arrangement viewed from the side are designed to help you avoid falling into this trap.

14. Plant material known as filler is used to cover the mechanics which should not be seen when the arrangement is finished.

15. The size and shape of the container must always be considered when choosing the plant material and the style of the arrangement. The container and the finished arrangement must appear as one complete unit and not two separate parts.

16. If any of the plant material is top heavy, some of the side shoots can be carefully cut away and the prunings so removed used lower down in the arrangement when filling in. Make sure, however, that the cuts are not noticeable in the finished arrangement.

17. Whenever possible try to arrange flowers where they will finally be viewed. It is then much easier to take into consideration their setting.

Facing arrangement in a tazza

The symmetrical facing arrangement can be created in a variety of containers but I shall explain in detail how to do it in a tazza as this is one of the easiest for a beginner to use. Place a medium-sized pinholder in the tazza about three-quarters of the way back in the centre, then fit in the wire netting as explained in the first section. I have chosen five different kinds of flowers in two colours to show the groupings more clearly. The pointed flowers are a bunch each of pink larkspur and white campanula and the round ones are five white carnations and seven pink roses. Three pink peonies have been selected to give weight in the centre of the arrangement. I have grouped the white flowers together to follow one direction through the arrangement and the pink flowers will go the opposite way. For the foliage, I have selected escallonia to go with the pink flowers and senecio with the white and I also have three large hosta leaves for the centre.

When you have prepared the flowers and the container and are ready to begin, select a campanula with a comparatively small flower. This will be the tallest stem and its height should be at least one-and-a-half times the height of the container and preferably twice. Secure this flower three-quarters of the way back in the centre of the container. All the facing arrangements which I shall describe, be they symmetrical, asymmetrical or L shaped, start three-quarters of the way back in the container. This is because if the arrangement were to start at the back of the container, the flowers which would be necessary to fill the space and come well out over the front edge would appear to bulge in the centre and the shape would be lost.

After you have positioned this first flower, take a second campanula with a slightly larger flower but a shorter stem and place this a little to the left side of the first campanula so that it is secured through the same hole of the netting and is adjacent to the first stem on the pinholder. Next take a small larkspur, cut it a little shorter than the second campanula and place it to the other side (right) of the first campanula, again securing it through the same hole of netting.

Establish the widest points on each side of the arrangement so that the overall width is roughly the same as the height. It is important to choose flowers which have curved stems so that they arch over the edge and join the arrangement with the tazza. In this way the flowers and the container appear as one unit and not two separate parts. Place a campanula on the opposite side to the second campanula, thus following the line of the grouping through, and a larkspur on the other side. Both these stems should be three-quarters of the way back in the tazza and of equal length. They should be as horizontal as possible but be well into the water.

All the stems in this arrangement, as indeed in any other, must appear to radiate from the tallest. However, they should not all touch it and some, especially those which form the outline, should only go half way towards it. If all the stems were to extend back to the tallest, this would lead to such a tremendous confusion and crossing of stems that a successful arrangement would be impossible to achieve.

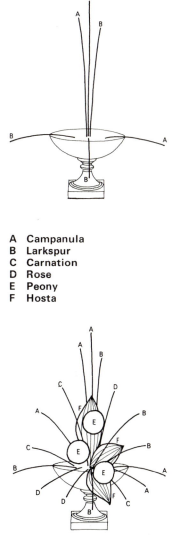

A Campanula
B Larkspur
C Carnation
D Rose
E Peony
F Hosta

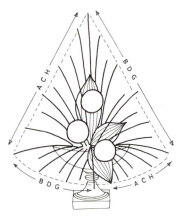

When you have positioned the stems demarcating the width, place a small pointed flower—I have used a larkspur—over the centre front edge of the tazza in line with the tallest campanula at the back. This becomes the longest flower at the front of the arrangement and completes the positioning of the main outline flowers. None of the subsequent stems should exceed these in length or the shape of the arrangement will be lost.

Proceed by joining up these principal outline flowers around the edge, remembering to keep your flowers in their groups. In this case the white flowers extend from high on the left to low on the right with the pink larkspur and roses arranged in the opposite direction. Bring the stem lengths down quite quickly at the back to achieve a triangular rather than a fan shape and make a good semi-circle around the front. Aim for a broken line around the edge with plenty of variation in stem length to prevent the arrangement from becoming too set.

Now that the outline is completed, place in some of the foliage. Keep the escallonia and rose foliage with the larkspur and roses and the senecio with the white flowers and follow the line of the flowers through, placing some foliage fairly high and some low to cover the netting. You will find that it is easier to fill in with foliage and cover the netting as you are doing the arrangement rather than leaving this important part until you have nearly finished.

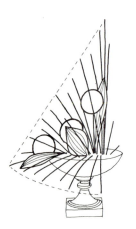

The peonies and hosta leaves are used to give a heart to the arrangement and are positioned next. The large centre flowers should not be kept in a straight line but should be arranged in zig-zag fashion. Only three large centre flowers are being used for this particular arrangement but often five or even seven are incorporated. The important thing is to get a good balance. Although an arrangement needs weight in the centre, the effect should not be too heavy. The large leaves are positioned to frame the main flowers and an uneven number is again used to prevent the arrangement from appearing too regimented.

Place the largest peony low into the centre with a smaller one above the first and a little to the right. The third peony goes low over the right front edge. The leaves should be positioned so that one goes over the right front edge, one goes at the back facing the one at the front and the largest leaf goes low into the centre and it should be turned slightly sideways.

It is essential that the groups of flowers should be connected through the centre so that they merge together, and here are a few words of advice which will apply to all arrangements. Good variation of stem length is important. Never have two flowers of the same length side by side. The smaller flowers should have the longer stems and be positioned high through the arrangement whereas the stems of the larger flowers should be cut so that they can be placed lower into the arrangement. Be careful not to make the arrangement look flat when it is viewed from the side. Even from this angle it should still present a triangular appearance as can be seen from the line drawing. Position some of the flowers so that their heads are facing sideways as this creates a more natural effect. None of the flower stems must cross one another and they must all appear to radiate from the base of the tallest.

When all the flowers are in position, check that the netting is covered, especially at the back, so that if the arrangement is seen from the side it will not present an unfinished appearance. The netting should be covered with short pieces of foliage. Some longer pieces can be used to cover the stems of the flowers and disguise the stalky effect which might develop. Do not overdo the foliage, however, as this might ruin the whole arrangement.

Study the arrangement by standing away from it. Make any necessary adjustments and top the tazza up to the rim with water from a small watering-can or something similar.

All-round arrangement

In my description of the method for doing this type of arrangement, I have used a silver dolphin container but you could do exactly the same arrangement in a flat bowl. A small pinholder is needed for the centre of the container over which the wire netting should be secured. There are five garnette roses of the variety Carol, nine mauve cornflowers, nine of the side stems of delphinium, five mauve freesia and twelve pieces of escallonia. The pointed subjects in an all-round arrangement, like the delphiniums in this one, should be generally short, otherwise they will give the finished arrangement a spiky appearance.

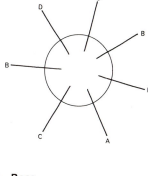

A Rose
B Cornflower
C Escallonia
D Freesia
E Delphinium

The foliage for this arrangement must be small so that it does not overpower the flowers or the container and I have chosen trails of leaves from pot plants—zebrina, variegated ivy in a grey tone and five pieces of sedum in a grey-green colour so that all the foliage is of a mauve or grey colouring. Also included are a few rose leaves to place in low with the rose group.

For an all-round arrangement, I find it easier to establish the shape around the edge of the container first. This is done by having an uneven number of outline points. In this arrangement I have seven but a smaller arrangement would only need five whereas a large one would take nine or even eleven. The more outline points used the easier it is to get a good shape. For the outline flowers I have chosen one rose, two escallonia, one delphinium, two cornflowers and one freesia.

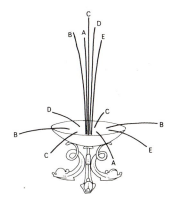

It is preferable to introduce each kind of flower into the outline though this is not possible when a particularly short-stemmed variety of flower is being used. The outline flowers chosen should be the smaller ones of each variety as this keeps the arrangement lighter around the edge. All the outline stems must be exactly the same length from the edge of the container to the top of the flower in order to ensure that the round shape is kept. They should also be placed roughly the same distance apart. If two of each kind of flower are being used to create the outline then they should be on opposite sides of the arrangement. However, if fewer varieties of flowers are being used, three of one kind may be needed on the outline. In this case place one flower on one side and two adjacent diagonally opposite. Should the outline contain four of a kind, place two adjacent on one side of the arrangement and the other two diagonally opposite to these. The flower stems go horizontally into the container about half way into the centre. They must, of course, be below the water line. The flowers should extend well over the edge of the container but not so far as to overpower it. For the size of this dolphin container, which is

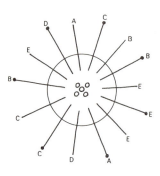

approximately four inches in diameter, about two inches over the edge is sufficient. The size of the arrangement is obviously related to the amount of plant material available but always allow the flowers to overlap the container. Never stop at the rim as this will give a stuffed appearance and the arrangement will not flow well. All the flowers in an all-round arrangement should be aimed towards the centre.

When the main outline flowers have been placed in position, the height must be determined. In a small arrangement like this the height can be the same as the overall width. The flower chosen to establish the height needs to be small and if possible pointed. I have chosen a piece of escallonia which is pink and will show up better than a blue or mauve flower. The height can vary according to where the finished arrangement is to be placed. For a table arrangement it needs to be kept low so that it does not block the view of anyone.

When the tallest flower has been placed in position and firmly established on the pinholder, place a few flowers of various kinds around and close to it. None of them must be as tall and each one needs to be a slightly different length. Usually four flowers around this centre one are sufficient to create a pretty pointed top to the arrangement. The width and the height of the arrangement will now have been established and none of the subsequent flowers or leaves must go beyond these points or the shape will be lost.

Now go back to the outline flowers around the edge of the container and place flowers of varying lengths between them. They need to be practically as long as the main outline flowers but do not place all of them to exactly the same length as you will then achieve the effect of a circle within a circle. A less set pattern is required. Conversely if these flowers are cut too short and placed in against the rim of the bowl, a star-shaped arrangement will be made and not a round one. It is very important when you are creating an all-round arrangement to keep turning the container round all the time. The danger is that you will complete one side and not have enough flowers left over to do the other. You may also end up with a very uneven effect.

The grouping of the flowers should run from one side to the diagonally opposite side i.e. roses opposite roses, escallonia opposite escallonia, delphiniums opposite delphiniums and so on. When looking down on to the top of the arrangement, however, the flowers should not be seen in a straight line across the bowl. There should be a slight zig-zag effect across to the opposite side. One flower group can merge with the flower group beside it e.g. a delphinium can merge in with the roses so that the flowers do not look too set like slices of cake. The foliage should be grouped with the flowers and some must be used to cover the netting. I have rose leaves with the roses, zebrina with the delphiniums, ivy with the cornflowers, sedum with the escallonia and freesias. In this way the foliage and flowers in each group complement one another. The zebrina foliage is fairly solid against the light delphiniums. The ivy looks well with the cornflowers and some of it can be used to trail over the edge of the container to connect it to the arrangement.

Connect up the flower groups in the arrangement, placing the larger heads lower down. Do not place any of the same kind of flower in a straight line and merge the groups well together. Keep

turning the arrangement around all the time and fill in with foliage where there is netting showing. Do not overcrowd the flowers as each should be clearly seen. Finally, top the container up to the rim with water.

Table centre in a trough

There are many trough-like containers available and even an oblong glass dish from the kitchen would be suitable. The container which I have selected is a rectangular shallow Denby-ware dish. I have placed a small square of Oasis in the centre of the dish under the wire netting but a pinholder would serve equally well.

I have chosen apricot and orange shades to achieve an autumnal effect. Pointed flowers are scarce when chrysanthemums and dahlias are available in the autumn and, as gladioli would be far too heavy for this table centre, I have selected fifteen montbretia. If you are unable to get pointed flowers then autumn berries are an excellent substitute. In fact, I have also chosen nine stems of hypericum berries to balance the montbretia and there are three berried sprays of viburnum and three of berberis. The round flowers consist of two stems of single and three stems of double chrysanthemum sprays with five each of two kinds of dahlia. The individual flowers from the sprays of chrysanthemums can be used singly.

The seedheads of physalis—Chinese lanterns—are particular favourites of flower arrangers and I have three sprays. I have removed the leaves from the stems as they are rather overpowering and tend to hide the lanterns. The foliage chosen includes nine apricot-coloured peony leaves, three sprays of autumn-coloured azalea leaves and five pieces of epimedium.

Begin with the flowers which will mark the length and choose those with curved stems so that the arrangement becomes linked to the container. Various factors including the size of the table, the number of flowers available and the size of the trough will determine how far these end stems should project over the edge of the container. The projection, however, should be the same either side. Two montbretias and one spray of hypericum should be placed on the left-hand side with one montbretia and two hypericum sprays on the right. The stems in each group should be of slightly varying length with a montbretia as the longest on the left and a hypericum as the longest on the right. The flowers in each group should be placed close together with the secondary stems of both the montbretia and hypericum at each end of the

A **Montbretia**
B **Hypericum**
C **Single chrysanthemum**
D **Double chrysanthemum**
E **Dahlia**
F **Dahlia**

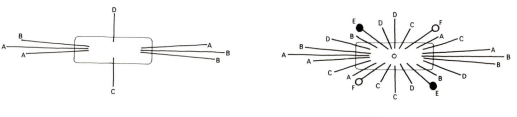

container positioned diagonally opposite each other. All these stems should appear to radiate from the centre but they should only go halfway towards it so that they are secured through the netting but not necessarily into the Oasis.

A small individual flower of a single chrysanthemum marks the widest point on one side of the width, with an individual flower from a double chrysanthemum spray on the other. These should not project over the edge as much as the flowers at either end of the length because the rectangular shape of the container needs to be taken into consideration. I have used an individual bud from a double chrysanthemum spray to establish the height. Its straight stem needs to be secured into the middle of the Oasis. As this arrangement is for a table centre, its height should not obscure the view of anyone across the table. Make a cluster of flowers around this chrysanthemum, keeping them close together and making each one a different length so that the arrangement is quite pointed in the centre. Introduce, if possible, each kind of flower including one of each kind of dahlia.

Next return to the edge and connect up the main outline flowers with a broken line of flowers and berries. The flowers are grouped with the single chrysanthemums and montbretia together and the double chrysanthemums and hypericum together. Keep turning the arrangement all the time and ensure that the groupings go diagonally across the trough. The flower heads, when arranged, should gently curve round between the outline points maintaining a broken line. As the dahlias are the largest flowers they should be positioned near the centre of the arrangement. One kind is grouped with the montbretia and single chrysanthemums and the other with the hypericum and double chrysanthemums. Position two of each type with their groups near the centre on the outline edge on either side of the trough.

Cover the netting with some of the foliage and bring some out over the edge of the container, then place in some of the berried subjects. The azalea, berberis and viburnum is grouped with the montbretia and single chrysanthemums and the Chinese lanterns and peony foliage with the double chrysanthemums and hypericum. Where there are only three pieces of a particular plant, place one on the edge on each side of the arrangement with the third quite near the centre. The lighter pieces of foliage and berries should be kept higher in the arrangement with the heavier pieces lower.

The remaining two dahlias of each type should be positioned so that there is one between the one on the edge and the centre one on either side and in either group. They should not be in a straight line but zig-zagged through the centre. Use the buds of the dahlias to lighten the arrangement.

Connect up the groups of flowers and merge them slightly through the centre. Check to see that the netting is covered and top up to the rim with water.

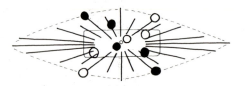
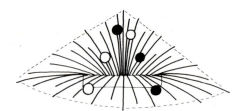

L-shaped arrangement

These arrangements can be quite narrow in width and so they are useful for mantelpieces. They can also be positioned on the chancel steps in a church or on window-sills. Pairs can be arranged with the height on the right of one and on the left with the other. You may find it easier to do an L-shaped arrangement with the height on one particular side.

Troughs or low oval containers are the best for these arrangements. They will never look happy in vases with stems. My container is a black oval trough in heavy pottery. The summer flowers are blues and greens. There are nine stems of blue delphiniums, five blue irises, two bunches of blue cornflowers, twelve stems of *Alchemilla mollis* and some euphorbia. For the foliage I have chosen stripped lime and three lime-green hosta leaves. With this plant material I have a good variety of shape.

Fit your container with wire netting and place a pinholder in the left-hand corner for the taller stems. Three-quarters fill the trough with water. Begin three-quarters of the way back and just in from the left-hand side. Secure a fairly straight piece of lime on to the pinholder. Ideally it should curve towards the left. Place a second shorter stem of lime to the left of the first and close into it. Establish the widest point on the right with a further stem of lime again securing it three-quarters of the way back in the container. This stem should curve naturally towards the surface on which the trough is standing and it should be roughly the same length as the tallest lime. A second shorter piece should be placed just in front of this one.

Next go back to the top of the arrangement and place a piece of alchemilla close to and shorter than the first lime and to the right-hand side of it. Then position another alchemilla low on the left-hand side. This will be the widest point here and it should project a little way over the edge of the trough. Place it in as horizontally as possible so that it connects trough and arrangement and secure it three-quarters of the way back making sure that it is in the water. Flowers will be placed into the arrangement so that they graduate from the tallest stem to this widest one and so the stem length of this alchemilla must be long enough to accommodate them. A third alchemilla becomes the longest flower in the front in line with the tallest lime at the back. All the stems should radiate from the tallest stem though they should not touch it. If they did then you would not be able to position the centre flowers and leaves. They should go far enough into the trough to be able to drink sufficient water.

Start to place in the main flowers. Because the blue delphiniums are light in colour, pointed in shape and straight stemmed, place one of these so that it is taller than the tallest lime. A second shorter delphinium should go to the left of this flower with a cornflower to the right, a little shorter still. Place another delphinium close to the widest lime on the right-hand side, a little shorter than it. You will then have completed the basic outline which should not be exceeded.

Finish this outline by placing the various groups around the edge with the smallest of each variety at the very edge, working the larger ones into the centre. From high on the left to low on the right go the lime, delphiniums and euphorbia. Retain the shape of

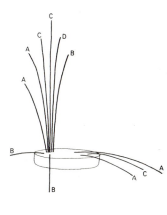

A Lime
B Alchemilla
C Delphinium
D Cornflower
E Iris
F Hosta

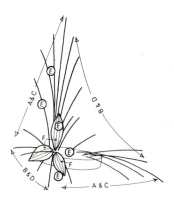

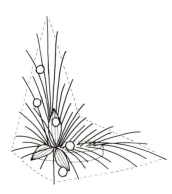

the L by graduating these stems quickly from the tallest to the widest and bring the front ones well out around the edge. Arrange the alchemilla and cornflowers through the other way. A mixture of these two flowers should come around the front edge to meet up with the longest piece of alchemilla at the front. The flowers in the second group should be kept very short at the back edge to maintain the L shape. Make sure that there is a good variation of stem length in the outline so that you achieve a broken effect.

The blue irises are the centre flowers. These should tend to go in the same direction as the lime and delphiniums but should be kept nearer the centre. Place the first iris—one with a small flower and long stem—to the left side of the second delphinium. Then go to the opposite front edge and position a second small iris. These two flowers might still be in bud. A third iris should be placed in between these two in the centre of the container. The position of the fourth iris is between the centre and front ones but slightly to the right of both and shorter in the arrangement. The fifth iris should be placed between the tallest at the back and the centre one but slightly to the left of both of them and again shorter into the arrangement.

The three hosta leaves frame the irises. A small one should go under the iris at the front edge. Another small one goes at the back facing this one with the largest leaf a little to the side and low into the centre. Turn this leaf slightly sideways.

Then place some of the other foliage, together with the shorter alchemilla, to cover the netting. Connect up the groups through the centre and make sure that the flowers do not overshadow the outline. Some of the larger flowers can go very short into the arrangement but even with these try to get variation in stem length. The left of the arrangement, where the height is established, is the only place where the flowers can be built out as in a facing arrangement. Face some of the flowers sideways to add interest. Do not overcrowd the plant material and distribute it equally. Make sure that the netting is covered at the back of the arrangement and top up with water.

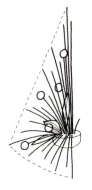

Off-centre facing arrangement

This arrangement could be described as a cross between the basic facing and the L shaped. Many would call it asymmetrical but I prefer to call if off-centre facing. The tallest flower is not in the centre but about a quarter of the way in from either the right or left-hand edge of the container. A variety of containers could be used although baskets and boxes with lids should be avoided and the urn shape is perhaps too narrow at the top to show the flowers to their best advantage.

I have selected a silver meat cover which has had a wrought-iron stand made for it. Its broad oval shape makes it especially suitable for this type of arrangement. The flowers are white ones which look restful and cool in hot weather. The sprays of philadelphus have had some of the leaves removed from around the flowers to prevent wilting. Beware, however, of removing too

Facing arrangement in a tazza

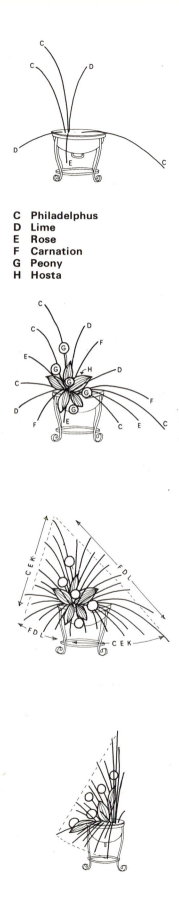

C **Philadelphus**
D **Lime**
E **Rose**
F **Carnation**
G **Peony**
H **Hosta**

many leaves as this would detract from the attractiveness of the spray. Stripped lime is grouped in the opposite way to the philadelphus. Eleven roses make up the round flowers with the philadelphus and there are eleven carnations grouped with the lime. For the filler there is alchemilla with the philadelphus and roses and periwinkle (vinca) with the lime and carnations. Five white peonies are the main centre flowers with five large variegated hosta leaves.

A small piece of well-soaked Oasis has been placed to the left-hand side of the container. I have chosen Oasis in preference to a pinholder as a screw from the handle has made the bottom of the meat cover uneven. The wire netting over the Oasis is secured to the wrought-iron stand in four places.

Begin with the outline flowers three-quarters of the way back in the container and a quarter of the way in from the left-hand side. Use a spray of philadelphus as the longest stem. This can curve slightly to the left. A second shorter piece of philadelphus can then be placed to the left of this, curving in line with the first. These two stems should be close together to obtain a pointed shape at the top. A stem of stripped lime is placed to the other side of the tallest philadelphus, again close to it and curving away from the centre. To define the width on the right side use a piece of philadelphus. This side is longer than the left and the stem should project well over the edge of the container with a downward curve. Also, because the meat cover is oval, the width of the finished arrangement should be slightly greater than the height. A piece of lime is used to mark the widest point on the left-hand side and this should be placed so that it too curves downwards. For the centre flower over the front edge of the container I have used a small-flowered rose, in line with the tallest flower at the back.

Fill in between these outline flowers by grouping the philadelphus and roses high on the left and low on the right with the lime and carnations arranged in the opposite direction. One side of the triangle will be longer than the other in this arrangement and the stem lengths should be decreased fairly quickly at the back to avoid a fan shape. Again a broken line should be aimed at with plenty of variation in stem length. The front should be rounded in shape but again one side will be longer than the other.

Use the peonies and hosta leaves to give weight and interest in the centre. The peonies should be positioned as follows: a small flower with a longish stem near the back against the first piece of philadelphus but shorter than it; another small flower over the front edge of the meat cover to the right of the first rose and nearly as long; a third peony between these two which becomes the centre flower; a larger shorter-stemmed flower between the front peony and the third and to the right of both; the last between the longest at the back and the centre one, to the left of them both.

The hosta leaves are positioned so that a small one comes over the front edge near the front peony. A second, larger leaf should be placed nearer the centre and turned sideways with a third—again small and longer stemmed—near the back peony so that it faces the front leaf. Another large one should be turned slightly and placed to one side of this with the fifth and largest leaf facing sideways in the centre.

Use some of the foliage to cover the netting, keeping the alchemilla with the philadelphus group and the vinca with the lime. Some of the rose leaves could be used with the roses. Connect the two groups through the centre and again have plenty of variation of stem length, with the flowers evenly spaced and not too close together. Turn some of the flowers sideways to add interest and keep the larger ones lower in the arrangement. Check to see that all the netting is covered and fill the container up to the rim with water.

Facing arrangement in an urn

Although this arrangement is similar to the facing arrangement in a tazza which I have already described, I have included it in my eight basic arrangements because the shape of the urn demands that the proportions are different. The urn is in grey pottery and because this container is comparatively tall and thin, it only needs wire netting in which to secure the flowers. Neither a pinholder nor Oasis are necessary.

I have chosen flowers in clashing reds—blue-reds and yellow-reds. There are fifteen stems of kaffir lilies which are pointed in shape and blue-red. The other pointed flower is orange montbretia. There are also two stems of red spray chrysanthemums, five dark red dahlias, three pieces of mountain spinach, three pieces of pyracantha with orange-red berries, five stems of wild rose hips, three pieces of bryony, three pieces of honeysuckle berries and three stems of skimmia berries. The foliage is in autumnal shades— seven stems of prunus and five pieces of *Ajuga repens atropurpurea*. There are also three bergenia leaves for the centre.

Begin this arrangement by placing a stem of montbretia, which measures between one-and-a-half times and twice the height of the urn, three-quarters of the way back in the centre of the container. Place a shorter-stemmed kaffir lily to the right of this and another montbretia to the left. These three flowers should be close together, so secure them through the same hole in the netting.

Next the width of the arrangement should be established by placing a curved-stem montbretia low down on the right-hand side, three-quarters of the way back in the container. The stem of this flower should be fairly short so that the finished arrangement echoes the elegant shape of the urn. The overall width of an arrangement in an urn should be a little over half the height. On the opposite side place a kaffir lily which is the same length as the montbretia on the right-hand side. Another montbretia should be brought well out over the front of the container in line with the tallest flower at the back. The main outline flowers will now be in position and, as with all arrangements, all the subsequent stems should appear to radiate from the tallest at the back. This is a little more difficult with a narrow-necked vase.

Introduce the berries into the arrangement and secure all the material used to fill in the back outline three-quarters of the way back in the container. Graduate the length of the stems down quite quickly at the back edge to avoid a rounded top. Create a good semi-circle around the front edge extending from the widest-placed flowers to the longest at the front. I have grouped the

A Montbretia
B Kaffir lily
C Dahlia
D Bergenia

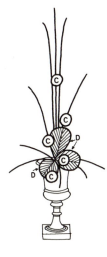

All-round arrangement

36

Top Table centre in a trough. *Bottom* L-shaped arrangement   37

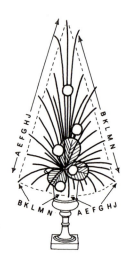

A Montbretia
B Kaffir lily
C Dahlia
D Bergenia
E Chrysanthemum
F Pyracantha
G Bryony
H Skimmia
J Prunus
K Hips
L Mountain spinach
M Honeysuckle
N Ajuga

montbretia and chrysanthemums with the berries of pyracantha, bryony and skimmia and the foliage of prunus high on the left and low on the right and the kaffir lilies, hips, mountain spinach, honeysuckle berries and ajuga high on the right and low on the left.

Place some of each kind of flower and berry in the outline but keep particularly curved stems like those of the bryony at the front edge of the arrangement and lower down. The straighter-stemmed hips will look well at the back and any curved stems of hips can be used to fill in the outline on the left-hand front edge.

When you have achieved a satisfactory outline put in the main flowers. A fairly small dahlia should be placed high but centred in the arrangement with another small flower to the left of the centre flower at the front. Zig-zag the other dahlias to meet up with these two flowers but keep them close through the centre. The three bergenia leaves are used to frame the dahlias. One should go over the edge at the front left; another, the largest, turned sideways in the centre; and the third should be placed at the back of the arrangement facing the one at the front.

At this stage fill up with foliage to cover the netting, keeping the prunus high on the left and low on the right, and the ajuga the opposite way. Connect up the groups of flowers and berries remembering to turn some of the plant material sideways to keep the arrangement looking more natural. When there are only three pieces of a particular flower to be used, as there are in several cases in this arrangement, have one high at the back of the arrangement, one low over the opposite side and one in the centre. Try to get good variation of stem length with the long stems bearing the smaller flowers and the shorter stems the larger ones. Do not make the main flowers in the centre look too obvious but merge the groups through them. If the centre flowers stand out too much the eye will rest on them and this will spoil the effect of the composition.

Finish by checking that the netting is covered and fill the urn up with water.

Facing arrangement in a basket with a handle

When creating an arrangement in a basket with a handle every care must be taken to ensure that the handle, or at least part of it, is seen when the arrangement is completed.

My basket has a baking-tin lining and this has been fitted with wire netting and a fairly large pinholder placed three-quarters of the way back in the centre to hold the heavier and longer stems.

I have chosen spring flowers because their yellow colouring and informality complement the colour and nature of the basket. To give added interest with the daffodils, narcissi and tulips, I am using some branches of hazel catkins and forsythia. These lend their pointed shapes to be grouped with the rounded flowers of the daffodils and tulips. The arrangement requires one-and-a-half bunches of large yellow daffodils, one-and-a-half bunches of the orange-centred narcissus Fortune and one bunch of the narcissus Soleil d'Or. This last variety is distinctive with several small flowers to each stem and provides a different shape. The five yellow tulips are treated as the main centre flowers and the foliage is tree ivy, trailing ivy and five bergenia leaves.

The main outline points are established with the hazel and forsythia. The height is determined by a piece of forsythia which should be placed so that it comes above the handle, to the left side of it and close in to it, three-quarters of the way back in the basket. It may be necessary to make the branches of forsythia and hazel less heavy at the top by pruning some of the sprigs away. This will help to keep the arrangement lighter at the top and a better shape. Pieces cut away from a branch can be used later in the arrangement in helping to cover the wire netting. Place a second, shorter piece of forsythia next to the first, again on the left side of the handle. A twig of catkins is placed on the opposite side to the first forsythia and to the right of the handle. This should be shorter than the second forsythia. If these stems have a natural curve use them so that they turn away from the centre of the basket. Never allow the branches to curve into the centre as they will then cross the stems of the centre flowers and will not appear to radiate from the tallest branch.

Determine the width of the arrangement by placing a piece of forsythia on the right and a twig of hazel catkins on the left. The length of these stems should be such that the overall width is slightly more than the height so that the shape of the finished arrangement is fairly low and flowing to echo the line of the container. Secure both these stems three-quarters of the way back in the container so that they come horizontally out over the edge of the basket. Place a piece of forsythia, which has been lightened by pruning, well over the front edge of the container so that it is on the opposite side of the handle to the tallest forsythia at the back. If this front piece is placed on the same side of the handle as the tallest branch, the arrangement would appear shorter on one side than the other and therefore unbalanced.

When you have established the main outline points, place more pieces of both forsythia and catkins around the edge to achieve a triangular rather than a fan shape. All the stems should radiate from the back but they should not touch the back stems as you will then have difficulty in positioning the flowers without moving the established points. Each stem should be placed so that its head is in the exact position where it is required. Do not place a stem and then try to move its head to a slightly different position.

The forsythia is positioned on the left side at the back of the basket and on the right side at the front, with the catkins placed in the opposite direction. Do not put in any pieces which are longer than the main outline or overshadowing it and aim for a semi-circular shape around the front of the basket.

Once the outline of twigs is in place, you can start to position the flowers. A comparatively small flower is needed as the longest one and I have chosen a small flower of Fortune. The second flower is a shorter-stemmed Fortune placed to one side of the first and both these flowers are positioned to the left of the handle. The third flower at the top is the smallest of the daffodils and this is placed to the right of the handle. A good guide to the length is to make each of these stems half a head shorter than the one before. The flowers marking the width are positioned next with a small Fortune, cut a little shorter than the forsythia, marking the

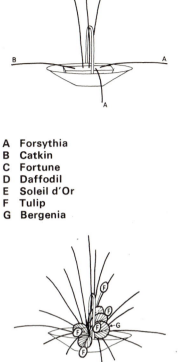

A   Forsythia
B   Catkin
C   Fortune
D   Daffodil
E   Soleil d'Or
F   Tulip
G   Bergenia

Top Off-centre facing arrangement. *Bottom* Facing arrangement in a basket with a handle

Facing arrangement in an urn

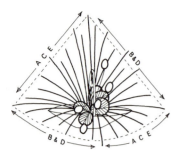

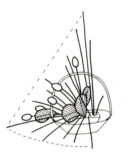

widest flower point on the right, and a small daffodil, a little shorter than the catkins determining the widest point on the left. Another small Fortune should be placed with the longest piece of forsythia in the front, on the same side of the handle. Again it should be cut a little shorter than the forsythia.

Next put in some flowers on the outline taking care to keep the shape established by the forsythia and catkins. The Soleil d'Or should be grouped in the same direction as the Fortune with the daffodils going the opposite way. When the outline is completed position the tulips. One should go at the back of the arrangement on the same side of the handle as the daffodils. Another goes over the front edge on the opposite side of the handle. The third is placed in the centre just above the handle so that it breaks the line of the handle slightly and makes a straight line with the first two tulips. The fourth tulip comes under the handle between the front tulip and the third tulip and the fifth is between the longest tulip at the back and the third. Do not place the fourth and fifth tulips in a straight line with the first three.

The five bergenia leaves are arranged near the centre with the tulips. The first, a small-sized one, should come over the front edge of the basket to the left of the handle. The second, a little larger, is placed further into the basket to the left side of the first and turned slightly to face the side. The largest, turned sideways, goes into the centre of the arrangement to the right with the fourth leaf at the back to the right of the handle and facing towards the first leaf. The last leaf should go a little further forward than the fourth, to the right and turned slightly sideways.

Next group some of the trailing ivy through the arrangement with the daffodils so that it comes well out over the edge of the basket and is high at the back. Use some shorter pieces through the centre. The tree ivy should be arranged in the opposite direction with the Fortune and Soleil d'Or.

Connect up the groupings so that they merge in the centre. Put some stems of forsythia and catkins through the arrangement and place some of the little pieces which have been trimmed away from the main stems lower down. The daffodil and narcissi leaves can be grouped in threes with differing lengths and five such bunches of these would be sufficient. The tulip leaves can also be used. It is possible to open one of the tulip flowers by turning back the petals and this creates the effect of a larger flower to give weight in the centre of the arrangement. Do not do this to any more, however, as it can look artificial. In order to keep the handle free, this arrangement is not built out to the same extent as the basic facing.

Finish, as usual, by checking the netting, especially at the back and top up the baking tin to the rim with water.

Line arrangement

Line arrangements should not be confused with Japanese flower arrangements. They are secured on to a pinholder which sits on a flat dish and are much simpler than the massed arrangements previously described. They generally contain only one type of flower and are very attractive in a modern home setting, although with care they can look equally well against traditional furniture.

This type of arrangement can be created with flowers alone but I especially like to add twigs. The branches for the arrangement shown here are those of the alder, cut before the catkin buds opened. There are also nine orange Apeldoorn tulips and five bergenia leaves which have a slight orange tinge to them.

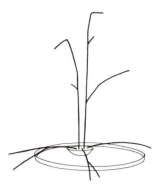

I have used a round woven tray for the base and on this has been placed, slightly to the left of centre, a small metal container to hold a large pinholder. Empty, painted salmon tins are particularly useful in this context if you have nothing else available. I have five pinky-orange pebbles to hide the metal container.

The outline is established with the alder. Choose a reasonably straight piece as the first and longest stem although a slight curve away from the centre at the top is an advantage. Secure this three-quarters of the way back on the pinholder in the centre. If this branch has another attached to it this may be considered as the second or third stem at the back of the arrangement depending on the length of this attached twig. Should it be necessary to trim away any side twigs, do this as close to the main branch as possible and try to have these cuts at the back of the branch when it is arranged. The light wood of a cut can look very ugly against the darker bark.

Next either position the second or third branch close to the first or both if the first branch had no convenient side twigs. The natural curve of these branches should be away from the centre.

The width is established by placing a piece of alder low to the left so that it comes over the edge of the tray and is close to it thus ensuring that the arrangement and tray become one unit visually. Position another stem of alder on the right-hand side but make sure that it does not project so far over the edge as that on the left. It is better if the finished arrangement does not look too symmetrical and it is for this reason that the water-holding container was put to the left of centre on the tray. The overall width should be slightly less than the height. A piece of alder should also be positioned in the front, in line with the tallest at the back.

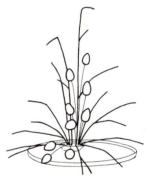

Fill in this main outline with alder at the back to achieve a triangular rather than a fan shape i.e. decrease the lengths of the stems quite quickly. Also connect the widest point to the centre taking care not to outstep the main outline. Vary the stem lengths to achieve a broken line and do not overcrowd them as it is important that the tray should be seen in the finished arrangement.

Now add the tulips. Take one with a small flower and a long stem. This may be difficult to find as inevitably it is the larger flowers which have the longer stems. However, it is essential to have a small flower as the longest at the back of the arrangement or it could easily look top heavy. Place this stem close to the longest alder and, if possible, it should curve in the same direction as this branch. A second tulip with a larger flower but shorter stem should then be positioned to one side of the first tulip, the same side as the second piece of alder. A third flower, larger and shorter stemmed still, goes to the other side. Each of these flowers is secured progressively a little further forward on the pinholder.

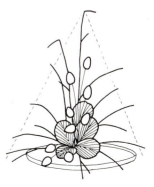

Next choose a small flower and secure this low at the front to the left of the front stem of alder and so that the flower touches

the edge of the tray. Place the stem sideways on to the pinholder. A second tulip with a larger flower and shorter stem should be positioned to the right of this front flower with a third, larger and shorter stemmed still, to the left of the front flower. These last two flowers are slightly higher than the first.

Then, in the centre, place three tulips to join the back and front groups together. A small-flowered, reasonably long-stemmed flower should be positioned in line with the flowers at the centre back and front. A larger, shorter-stemmed flower goes to the right of this one, further back on the pinholder with an even larger but shorter-stemmed flower to the left of centre and towards the front. When completed the tulip flowers should be equidistant. It is especially important in this type of arrangement to position the flowers exactly right as there are so few of them.

The five bergenia leaves are needed to give added weight in the centre and to frame the flowers, and these are positioned next. Place a small but long-stemmed leaf at the back near to the first tulip and reaching to about half way up its stem. Position another small leaf with a longish stem against the first flower at the front edge so that it is shorter than the tulip. A third leaf goes to the right of the first and shorter than it with a fourth of similar size to the left of the second. The fifth, largest leaf should be cut very short and placed sideways into the centre of the arrangement.

Put the finishing touches by placing more alder branches attractively between the tulips and if any of the pinholder or the container can be seen use some tulip leaves to cover them. Fill in the back of the arrangement with leaves, and finally arrange the pebbles from the edge of the tray towards the container so that the eye is carried through to the centre. Fill the container to the rim with water.

Line arrangement

VARIATIONS ON THE THEME

Cupid of lilies-of-the-valley

The container used in this arrangement is made of white china and it is fashioned in the shape of a cupid holding a shell. I adapted the basic facing arrangement but paid special attention to the height. The figure must not appear to be staggering under the weight of the flowers. It is the shape of the shell which needs to be considered keeping the arrangement fairly low and spreading. I used three bunches of lilies-of-the-valley, which included three leaves, and some green trailing ivy. The shell was fitted with wire netting and a small pinholder.

As for the basic facing arrangement, I began three-quarters of the way back in the centre with a small flower. This had a stem roughly equal to the height of the whole container. Then I placed in two further stems, one on either side of the tallest, with each a little shorter so that there were three different lengths with the flowers getting gradually larger. The width was established by using two stems of equal length, one either side. These were longer than those used for the height so that the shape of the shell was kept. The flower marking the centre front was short stemmed so that it did not hide the face of the cupid.

I then filled in between these main outline points, taking care to keep the shape, with a broken line along the front and back. The lengths of the stems were decreased quickly at the sides to avoid a fan shape. The three small lily-of-the-valley leaves were placed in position—one at the back, one over the edge at the front and the shortest one in the centre. I ensured that the leaves were not in a straight line by positioning the centre one slightly to one side.

The ivy was then trailed through the arrangement so that some pieces went over the edge of the shell. The remaining flowers were positioned evenly throughout and I made sure that although no stems were longer than the outline, there was plenty of variation in their length. To obtain a less formal effect, some shorter flowers of varying length were recessed behind the outline. The arrangement was finished by covering the netting at the back with ivy leaves before topping the container up to the rim with water.

This container could also be arranged with small mixed flowers and with an off-centre arrangement.

46

Cupid of lilies-of-the-valley

All-round arrangement of mixed garden flowers in a basket

For an arrangement such as this one, go into the garden and pick as many different flowers as you can. You do not need many of each kind—two or three would be sufficient. A good variety of shape and colour is important but avoid white and try to include yellow and/or lime green as these will bring out the colours of the other flowers. I chose yellow irises, blue delphiniums, red antirrhinums, mauve statice, purple flag irises, orange marigolds, mauve sweet peas, pink and red stock, red rhododendrons, red sweet williams, pink pyrethrums, lime-green *Alchemilla mollis*, and orange and yellow roses. The foliage was lamium and *Stachys lanata*. It is not necessary to use very much foliage in a mixed arrangement as, with so many flowers, the wire netting is soon covered.

The basket has a metal lining and I used wire netting with a pinholder under it in the centre. The wire netting was attached to the wickerwork round the edge of the basket so that the lining and basket were held firmly together.

The same principles apply to this arrangement as to the basic all-round one described in Section Two. The height should be roughly the same as the overall width. The flower marking the height should be small and of a light colour. Mine was a yellow iris and I cut the stem so that when positioned in the container, the flower came two or three inches above the handle. I used nine outline points which were two marigolds, two sweet peas, one statice, two red antirrhinums and two pink stock. With these in position I went back to the centre flower and placed around it further flowers of varying shape, colour and length. These were a blue delphinium, red antirrhinum, mauve statice, purple iris and alchemilla. The outline round the edge was then filled in and the flowers were grouped from one side to the opposite side in the same way as for the basic all-round arrangement. The other flowers were introduced at this stage and these were grouped too.

Next, I covered the netting with foliage, grouping the lamium one way and the *Stachys lanata* the other. The centre was gradually built up from one side to the other keeping the large flowers low in the arrangement and the small ones high and care was taken not to hide the handle of the basket. The two smallest pieces of rhododendron were placed one at either side at the edge and the third low in the centre.

When creating an arrangement of this kind mix the different coloured flowers well. Do not overcrowd the arrangement but leave a little space between each flower. All the stems should appear to radiate from the tallest flower in the centre. Keep turning the basket round all the time.

If a lower arrangement is desired, the tallest flower could come below the handle and all the flowers kept lower accordingly.

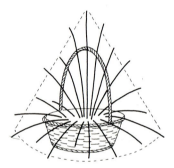

Table centre of roses in a silver cake basket

Roses often look more attractive when they are arranged on their own and it is always preferable to use their own leaves with them. If, however, they are poor and cannot be used, a more fussy foliage could be substituted. *Alchemilla mollis* is a particularly attractive filler for roses. Before arranging roses cut away some of their thorns to avoid damaging the leaves, and to make them more comfortable for you to handle.

For this arrangement I used an oval silver cake basket with an oval glass dish placed inside as a lining. Under the netting, in the centre, I placed a medium-sized pinholder to hold the heavier stems. After tying the netting into the glass dish, I also attached it in four places to the cake basket. This prevented the glass lining from moving.

The roses used were all pink ones—tints and shades of the one hue—and they were picked from the garden. You can, of course, use roses bought from a florist. I grouped pale pink Dr W. Van Fleet roses with garnette roses of the variety Carol and Constance Spry roses with darker pink roses. I was forced to include some of the Dr W. Van Fleet roses in this second grouping as there were not enough roses of the other two varieties to balance the first group.

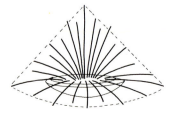

48   ***Top* All-round arrangement of mixed garden flowers in a basket**
***Bottom* Table centre of roses in a silver cake basket**

When arranging flowers in an oval dish you must always bear in mind the shape of the container and follow it. An oval can be said to have a length and width. For the two longest flowers in this arrangement I used a Dr W. Van Fleet at one end and at the opposite end the buds and flower of one of the darker pink roses. These both came about four inches over the edge. A shorter Dr W. Van Fleet was placed to one side of the first and diagonally opposite to it I placed a third Dr W. Van Fleet rose. As the third flowers at either end I used a fourth and fifth Dr W. Van Fleet rose. In theory these should perhaps have been Constance Spry roses but as I did not have many of these and they were all larger blooms I thought it better to substitute the smaller roses. In order to keep the oval shape, these first three flowers at either end were not placed so close together as the flowers in the long low table centre arrangement described in Section Two.

The widest points on either side were established by using a further two Dr W. Van Fleet roses and I used another of this variety with a fairly straight stem and small flower for the centre height. Beware of making such an arrangement too tall otherwise the view of your guests across the table may be blocked.

I then filled in the outline, grouping the flowers and being careful to keep the oval shape. The two groupings went diagonally across the arrangement. I went back to the centre and placed roses with stems of various lengths around the tallest flower before covering the netting with some of the rose leaves. Wherever possible I tried to keep the compound leaves of the roses intact.

I finally connected up the groups of roses. The roses with the smaller flowers had the longer stems and I cut down the stems of the larger blooms so that they were shorter. I also placed the darker flowers lower. Rose leaves with longer stems were placed through the arrangement but not so many as to overpower the flowers.

Chrysanthemums in a bronze urn

You may find difficulty in arranging the large chrysanthemum blooms of autumn and here is just one idea. You will need a heavy container to balance the weight of the flowers. I used a bronze urn and five of the apricot chrysanthemum Shantung. The foliage was three large bergenia leaves and some peony leaves which had turned their attractive autumn colour. As an alternative to these peony leaves you could use beech leaves which have been preserved in glycerine.

A piece of well-soaked Oasis was used under the netting in the urn to prevent the heavy blooms from moving. I positioned the chrysanthemums first, beginning with the smallest flower, the stem of which was cut so that when secured in the container it was one-and-a-half times the height of the urn. This first stem was placed three-quarters of the way back in the centre. A second small chrysanthemum was placed over the front edge of the urn and a little to the right. Next I positioned a third, slightly larger flower with a shorter stem to the left of the first flower, leaving a

small space between the two blooms. The fourth chrysanthemum, a little larger and shorter stemmed still, went to the other side of the first flower. The fifth and last chrysanthemum was positioned to the side of the front flower and short into the arrangement. The stems, from the back one to the front, were secured a little further forward in the netting.

The three bergenia leaves were placed so that one was over the front edge on the left side to balance the chrysanthemum on the right side. The second went towards the back on the right but facing towards the front leaf and the third and largest was placed in low on the opposite side of the urn to the fifth bloom and turned sideways.

The peony leaves marked the width. I did not make the arrangement very wide as the urn is fairly tall and the shape of the arrangement should enhance this. I also placed a peony leaf in the front of the container between the chrysanthemum and the bergenia leaf to mark the longest point at the front. More peony leaves were positioned at the back and low through the container to cover the netting.

Wooden box arranged with cream flowers

This arrangement was created in a converted writing box with a baking-tin lining. The baking tin was placed on blocks of wood so that its top edge was level with the top of the box. This is important because otherwise it is extremely difficult to get a good flow of flowers over the edge of the box. The lid should be lined with material to tone with the flowers and must be visible in the finished arrangement. This can be achieved in a variety of ways. The flowers could be arranged higher in the centre so that the two top corners are seen, or the lid could be half closed and the flowers arranged to spill out from under it. However, I prefer to adapt the basic L-shaped arrangement. A basket with a lid could be used instead of the writing box.

For this particular arrangement I chose to adopt a cream colouring and I lined the lid of the box with cream satin. The pointed flowers were cream broom and five cream stock. There were also ten single tulips, three double tulips and nine Roselandia roses—all single flowers on a stem and all a cream colour. Three straw-coloured hyacinths were selected to give weight in the centre of the arrangement and there were also three polyanthus and one bunch of the narcissus Yellow Cheerfulness, both with many flowers to a stem. The foliage and flowers used for filling in were golden philadelphus (*Philadelphus coronarius aureus*), three stems each of two kinds of spurge or euphorbia and three bergenia leaves.

I placed a pinholder in the left-hand side of the box and then put in my wire netting. Three pieces of broom of differing lengths established the height and I next added a stem of stock, keeping this fairly high and placing it near the centre of the broom. The overall width of such an arrangement needs to be roughly equal to the height. One of the smaller-flowered stocks was used to

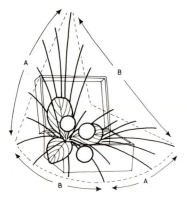

Wooden box arranged with cream flowers

53

mark the width on the right-hand side, placed so that it came well out over the edge of the box. A rose was used as the outline point on the left-hand side and although this went out over the edge of the box, it was not such a long projection as on the right-hand side. A narcissus became the longest flower over the front edge in line with the tallest flower at the back. I then returned to the height, placing a rose to the right-hand side of the stock and a tulip to the other.

The arrangement was filled in grouping the single tulips, stock and broom together high on the left and low on the right and the roses and narcissi went the other way. The flowers were brought well out over the edge. All the stems radiated from the pieces of broom at the back. The hyacinths, double tulips, and polyanthus were placed near the centre with the double tulips grouped with the single tulips, broom and stock and the polyanthus with the roses and narcissi. The hyacinths were central.

The netting was covered by foliage and some of the euphorbia and some leaves came well out over the edge of the container. The philadelphus was positioned high on the left side and low on the right together with one variety of euphorbia and some of the tulip leaves. The second kind of euphorbia and the rose leaves went the other way. I placed the bergenia leaves near the centre with the hyacinths. One went out over the front edge with the second near the broom at the back. The largest leaf was placed sideways and shorter into the centre. I finished the arrangement by connecting the various groups through the centre, placing some of the flowers sideways to give further interest. The flowers were evenly spread throughout and none of them overshadowed the outline.

Shell arrangement of bluebells and anemones

This shell can be used in various ways—for an arrangement to be seen from both sides, a centred facing arrangement or an off-centre facing arrangement and I think this last one is the most interesting. Whichever way is chosen, the shape of the shell must always be borne in mind and the arrangement kept fairly low and flowing. I chose wild bluebells with a mauve tinge, seven purple anemones, some tradescantia leaves and five small variegated *Hosta undulata* leaves. A pinholder was placed a little to the left side of the container under the netting. The outline flowers were all bluebells with the round anemones kept for the centre to give weight and to hold the arrangement together.

I began a little in from the left-hand side and three-quarters of the way back in the container with a small-flowered bluebell. I then placed a second and third bluebell to either side of this first one, each with a slightly larger flower and shorter stem. The width was determined with a long-stemmed small bluebell on the right and a shorter-stemmed small flower on the left. The longest flower over the front edge was, as usual, in line with the tallest flower at the back.

The main outline points were joined up and care was taken to

54

keep a broken line along the front and back edge and I placed the seven anemones through the centre of the arrangement keeping the weight towards the longest side. The five hosta leaves were positioned through with the anemones so that they framed the flowers. The smaller leaves went at the back and over the edge at the front and the larger leaves in the centre. The leaf at the back faced the one over the front edge and the centre ones were turned slightly sideways. The tradescantia was also placed in at this stage to help cover the netting.

The bluebells were placed from side to side through the arrangement from the back flower to the longest at the front edge. I merged these flowers in with the anemones and made sure that there was plenty of variation in the lengths of the stems. The arrangement was finished by covering the back netting with tradescantia.

Small china basket with handle

This type of arrangement is very useful for a bedside table and even though small it can contain a mixture of flowers. Often the side shoots from taller and bigger flowers will provide suitable material. A piece of well-soaked Oasis may be sufficient for a little container like this white china basket but netting can be used. It may in any case be safer to have a small piece of netting fastened over the Oasis to hold this steady.

I chose blue and white flowers—small side branches of philadelphus, some in flower and others with seedheads, white freesias, blue alpine campanulas, a few of the white pink Mrs Simpkins, and three dark blue cornflowers to give weight in the centre. The shape of the flowers in a small arrangement is still very important as is a good variety of foliage. I selected the bitty foliage of rue, the clean cut leaves of trailing ivy—these were both roughly the same weight—and three very small leaves of the variegated *Hosta undulata* for the centre. Since the container has a handle I had to bear this in mind throughout and, therefore, I adapted the basic arrangement for a basket with a handle.

A seedhead of philadelphus established the tallest point to the left of the handle. The second flower was a bud of Mrs Simpkins and this went to the right of the handle and it was a little shorter than the seedhead. A philadelphus flower was placed on the opposite side (left) of the tallest stem. All these flowers were three-quarters of the way back in the basket. To mark the width I used a philadelphus flower on the right-hand side and a freesia on the left. The width measured a fraction more than the height as the container is fairly low and wide. The longest flower over the front edge was a philadelphus and this went to the right of the handle—the opposite side to the tallest flower.

The outline was filled in by grouping the freesias, pinks and campanulas one way and the philadelphus—buds, flowers and seedheads—the other. The cornflowers were placed in the centre. One went just beneath the tallest pink, one over the front edge to the right of the handle and the third in the centre to the left

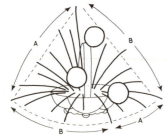

of the handle so that they were not in a straight line. The hosta leaves were placed to frame the cornflowers.

I grouped the rue with the freesias, pinks and campanulas to cover the Oasis and the ivy with the philadelphus. The flower groups were joined up so that the handle was still visible and there was variation in the stem lengths. The arrangement formed a triangle at the back and a semi-circle round the front. A final check to see that the netting was covered, especially at the back, was made and the container was filled up to the rim with water.

Pedestal arrangement

Pedestal arrangements are usually centre facing ones although off-centre ones can be very successful. You will need to consider the height of the pedestal and shape of the container and in order to maintain a sense of proportion between the arrangement and the stand, the arrangement may be narrower and taller than the basic arrangements. Pedestal arrangements are usually sited in large halls and churches and to make any impact they need to be larger than life. When decorating such big buildings, one large arrangement is better than many smaller ones.

You may need to use the tubes or cones described in the chapter on accessories to give extra height. If, however, the stems are long enough to go straight into the container, this is much better than using cones. An averaged-sized pedestal arrangement usually needs three cones. These should be placed in position first so that they are well anchored in the wire netting and also into the pinholder or Oasis underneath.

I used a block of Oasis when I created the pedestal arrangement illustrated here. I chose Oasis in preference to a pinholder because my container was a shallow bowl and the soaked Oasis added weight to give better balance. The Oasis did not completely fill the container but I left space to top up with water. Not all the stems went into the Oasis and some were only anchored into the wire netting round the edge. I was also wary of having the Oasis too high above the rim of the container as this would have encouraged me to place the stems in unnatural downward facing straight lines. Instead, gently curving stems should flow over the edge of the container.

I used three cones in this arrangement, each of a differing length with the tallest one in the centre, and they were secured three-quarters of the way back in the container. It is a good idea to place the sticks to which the cones are attached so that they touch one another as this makes for a more stable arrangement. The cones must be upright in order to hold the water and they should each be fitted with a small piece of wire netting.

For the flowers I used five arum lilies, five stems of white lilac, two bunches of white iris, seven stems of guelder rose, *Viburnum opulus*—I used these in the green stage as they last so much longer then—and seven white carnations. The foliage was elm, camellia and philadelphus and five arum lily leaves. The lilac, irises and camellia foliage were grouped from high on the right to low on the left with the guelder rose, carnations and philadelphus the opposite way. The arums and their leaves went in the centre to give weight there.

Before starting the arrangement, the cones were covered with the solid foliage of camellia and philadelphus. You will find that it is not always necessary to use the longest stemmed flowers in the cones. Shorter ones will often suffice as their height is provided by the cones. The longer-stemmed flowers can then be reserved for positioning straight into the container. Try, therefore, to avoid cutting down stems to put into the cones as long stems are essential to the success of these arrangements.

I began by achieving a rough outline with the prettily shaped elm twigs. These did not necessarily provide the longest outline material but they gave a general shape to work to. Three pieces of slightly different length went at the top with the longest piece in the middle cone, and the pieces either side in the other two cones. Another two pieces were placed in on either side to determine the width. These were curved to achieve a good flow over the edge and these stems went three-quarters of the way back in the container and radiated from the tallest. I connected up these points with further branches of elm—those at the back curving away from the centre.

The longest flower at the top came above the elm. This was a small-flowered lilac and it was secured in the middle cone. To the right of this in the right-hand cone I used a second, slightly shorter piece with a larger head. On the left of the tallest flower, in the left-hand cone, I placed the third longest flower—a small-headed guelder rose. The widest point on the left-hand side was marked with a small-headed lilac and that on the right with a piece of guelder rose. The stems of both these flowers curved over the edge of the container. The longest flower at the front was an iris.

Then I connected up the outline, keeping the flowers in their two groups so that they were evenly balanced. I kept to the shape defined by the elm and decreased the stem lengths quickly at the back to avoid a fan shape. An elegant shape is very important in a pedestal arrangement. Sprays of camellia were included with the lilac and iris to help cover the netting with some philadelphus in the other group. Foliage which curved well was used on the edge to connect the container and pedestal.

The arums were placed next. One went fairly high at the centre back of the arrangement just in front of the first piece of lilac; another went on the front edge to the right of the centre flower; a third went between these two in the centre. These three flowers were the smallest. The two largest went between the centre and tallest ones so that they were not in a straight line and the arum leaves were placed to frame their flowers.

The arrangement was finished in the usual way. The groups were connected through the centre with good variation in the length of the stems. Some of the flowers were turned sideways with the larger ones placed shorter into the arrangement. I checked to see that the netting was covered and filled the container up to the rim with water. With a pedestal arrangement it is important to see that the cones are well hidden and that they are full of water.

If creating an off-centre pedestal arrangement, work as for a basic off-centre facing but to a larger scale. Although I created this arrangement in a shallow bowl, a more upright container would have been equally as good. Pedestal arrangements need to be very well balanced and firmly secured so that there is no danger of them toppling over.

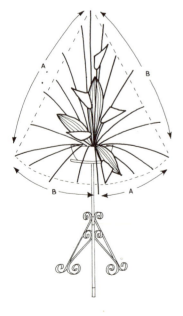

Pedestal arrangement

Dutch group

When creating this Dutch group arrangement, I did not copy a particular Dutch painting but I did take into account the colour, style and flowers used by the painters. The flowers I chose were one yellow fritillary, two yellow gladioli, two white ranunculus, three red ranunculus, three red border carnations, cherry blossom, malus blossom, one blue hyacinth, one blue iris, one stem of clivia, two purple tulips, two pink and white tulips, two stems of *Viburnum opulus* (guelder rose), two yellow roses, purple hellebores, three pheasant eye narcissi and *Viburnum tinus*. These provided a great variety of colour and shape.

The container, a black urn with a green tinge, was fitted with wire netting and as it is fairly deep it was unnecessary to use a pinholder or Oasis. I decided to use a picture frame to complete the effect. This has metal pieces at the back to enable it to stand up and from time to time, when I was establishing the outline, I placed the frame in front of the arrangement to make sure that all the flowers were fitting in.

I began as usual three-quarters of the way back in the container with a yellow gladiolus. I chose this flower because it was a pointed shape and the colour showed up well. A spray of cherry became the second flower and the other gladiolus was placed in front of this. On the opposite side (left) I used a small-flowered red ranunculus. A Dutch group requires a more rounded top than is usual for a facing arrangement. A stem of malus became the widest point on the right-hand side with a red border carnation on the other. For the longest flower at the front I used a purple hellebore.

With the main outline established, I placed the fritillary low into the right of centre with the clivia higher on the opposite side to balance it. When these larger flowers were in place, I finished the outline keeping a semi-circular shape at the front and also having the back fairly rounded. With a Dutch group it is not necessary to be particular with the grouping but the flowers should be well balanced and evenly spread through the arrangement. The *Viburnum tinus* was used to help fill in and also to cover the netting. Variation of stem length is still important with Dutch arrangements and it adds interest if you turn some of the flowers sideways. All the stems should radiate from the centre.

When the arrangement was finished, I placed a bird's nest by the urn to complete the effect. Nests were often painted into these pictures and they do add interest and weight to the base of the arrangement. Instead of a bird's nest, a shell could be used or, if you prefer, a preserved butterfly may be placed on to the arrangement itself. Sometimes an open rose or another flower was used at the base of the container. This type of arrangement would be suitable for a traditional setting and could be particularly effective if placed as a copy beside an actual painting or print.

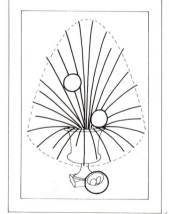

Peonies in a black dish

For this line arrangement in a black pottery dish, I used a large pinholder because peonies are heavy flowers and placed it in the right corner. You may want to use a dish which is too shallow to

hold water. If this is so, place a water-holding container on the dish and disguise it if need be with blocks of glass or pebbles. My dish was deep enough to hold water but I did use five blocks of glass to give a cool effect and to help cover the pinholder. The plant material consisted of seven red peonies with their own foliage.

My arrangement formed a backward L, going from high on the right to low on the left. As usual I began three-quarters of the way back on the pinholder with the tallest and smallest flower which in fact was a bud. A second larger and shorter-stemmed peony was placed to the right of the first and a little further forward. A third flower, a little larger and shorter stemmed still, was positioned on the opposite side of the first flower and secured a little further forward than the second flower on the pinholder.

The fourth peony with a small flower and curved stem was placed low on the left-hand side so that it went just over the edge of the dish and was anchored on the edge of the pinholder. I positioned the fifth flower a little higher than the fourth. It had a larger bloom but a shorter stem and was secured nearer the centre of the pinholder.

The sixth peony, which was large flowered, was placed into the centre of the arrangement, low on to the front edge and fastened at the front of the pinholder. In this way the flowers were worked down from the tallest and in from the widest. I placed the largest peony between these two groups of three, very short into the centre.

I filled in with peony leaves, some having been retained on the flowers. None projected much further than the flowers as this would have spoilt the line but I brought them through the arrangement and covered the pinholder at the back. The pieces of glass were placed just under the peonies with the largest one hiding the pinholder.

Facing arrangement in a copper pan

I have included this to show that facing arrangements need not be confined to containers with stems. This copper pan is suitable for quite large displays and it could be used on a pedestal. I chose it to complement the red flowers and berries and fitted it with a large pinholder and netting.

The flowers were five red gladioli, five of the red spray chrysanthemum Nero, five scarlet dahlias, seven darker red dahlias, three red standard chrysanthemums and seven red carnations. I also used haws and cotoneaster berries and the autumn foliage of prunus, wild guelder rose, nut and peony. The centre leaves were five of bergenia.

As for the basic arrangement, I used three flowers to mark the height—two gladioli and one spray chrysanthemum. The widest flower at the right side was a gladiolus and on the left a spray chrysanthemum. Spray chrysanthemums can be pruned down to make them lighter and the flowers so removed used low down in arrangements when filling in. The longest flower over the front was a spray chrysanthemum.

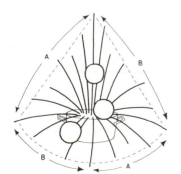

62

I grouped the gladioli, scarlet dahlias, carnations, nut, guelder rose and cotoneaster high on the left and low on the right, and the spray chrysanthemums, darker dahlias, haws, peony and prunus the opposite way. With the main outline completed, I filled in keeping the shape pointed at the back and rounded at the front. The centre flowers were then positioned and also the leaves—the standard chrysanthemums and bergenia leaves—before placing in some foliage to help cover the netting. With all the flowers radiating from the tallest gladiolus at the back and evenly spaced, I connected up the groups and merged them in the centre. I finished the arrangement by checking that the netting was covered and topped up the container with water.

This arrangement would be suitable for a traditional Christmas setting substituting holly and ivy for the foliage and berries.

L shape of mixed greens in a mirror trough

I have included this to show that effective arrangements can be created from greenery alone. These are especially welcoming in summer for the cool effect they give and they·are enhanced if placed so that they are reflected in a mirror. I used some green flowers but attractive results can be had from foliage on its own provided there is a good variety of shape, shade and texture. This arrangement was designed to half frame a mirror above a mantelpiece with some of the pieces trailing over the top of the mantelpiece.

The plant material included pointed flag iris leaves, the more solid leaf of elaeagnus, ivy, *Helleborus corsicus* flowers, sedum, the round head of angelica, bitty woad, *Stachys lanata*, *Begonia* Iron Cross with its interesting markings, bright green euphorbia, *Cassinia fulvida*, variegated rue and apple mint, large plain green hosta leaves and lime-green nicotiana.

My container is a mirror trough and I fitted it with wire netting and put a pinholder in the left-hand corner. The proportions were the same as those used in the basic L-shaped arrangement. For the height I used a flag iris leaf, securing it three-quarters of the way back in the container. A second flag iris leaf was placed a little to the right of the first and shorter. A stem of elaeagnus, shorter than the second flag iris leaf, was placed to the opposite side of the tallest leaf.

The widest point on the left-hand side was established with a piece of apple mint and on the right-hand side with a stem of euphorbia. A piece of woad became the longest stem at the front. I grouped the elaeagnus, rue, ivy, hellebores, sedum and euphorbia high on the left and low on the right and the apple mint, cassinia, woad, stachys and nicotiana the opposite way. The angelica head together with the begonia and hosta went in the centre.

It is more difficult to get the effect of variation in stem length with foliage so I emphasised this aspect with the flowers. I was, however, careful to keep the L shape by making the stems at the right back very short. I finished by covering the netting at the back and topping up with water.

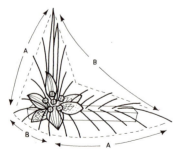

Top L shape of mixed greens in a mirror trough
Bottom Wicker trough with spring flowers

Wicker trough with spring flowers

This very informal arrangement, which was designed for a luncheon party, looks most attractive when simple country or even wild flowers are used. My flowers were seventeen pheasant eye narcissi, nine Christmas roses, *Helleborus niger*, and five bunches of snowdrops. Small tree ferns which grow on walls the whole year round, some tree ivy leaves with their berries and bun moss provided the greenery. The container has a lining and I fitted it with netting, keeping this high so that the bun moss was kept out of the water. Two medium-sized pinholders were placed under the netting about a quarter of the way in from either side. The netting was attached to the basket in four places and this secured the lining firmly to the basket.

The flowers were not arranged as such but placed in clumps of their own type as if they were growing. You could use more kinds of flower to give greater variety or, if preferred, only one type of flower need be chosen. The container was three-quarters filled with water and the netting covered with moss which was kept fairly level. Where the moss was too thick, I cut away some of the fibres from the back. I made sure that the moss was not touching the water as it can act as a syphon.

Two clumps of narcissi were placed one on either side of the trough, one group being taller than the other. None of the narcissi, however, was more than nine inches high as the arrangement was to be used as a table centre. I parted the moss in order to position the narcissi and included some of their leaves in each clump. The flowers were arranged to face in all directions and they stood straight to look as if they were growing. There was variation in the stem lengths in each clump.

The hellebores were placed in three groups. The first clump was positioned sideways over the right edge (i.e. to the right as the arrangement is shown here) to break the line of the trough and the second group served a similar purpose diagonally opposite. These two groups were not identical, however, as the arrangement must appear natural and not too set. The third clump connected the grouping in the centre of the container between the narcissi.

There were five groups of snowdrops which began on the 'left' of the trough on one side and these were worked towards the opposite edge. For this the flowers were retained in their original bunches and the cotton which tied them together was simply loosened. I also included some snowdrop leaves with each group.

There were three clumps of both the ivy and ferns which served to break the line of the container and add interest. They also added extra length. I checked to see that the bun moss covered the netting and filled the container to the rim with water.

Arrangement in green urn

This arrangement is a different shape to any of the others previously described in the book. The tallest stems are in the centre but the

sides although balanced in weight are off balanced in shape. The container is a tall urn of a yellowy-green colour and I used flowers of a lime-green colour. There were five Woodpecker gladioli, three fatshedera leaves, some *Alchemilla mollis* and some attractively curved stripped lime.

I began three-quarters of the way back in the container and in the centre with a small-flowered gladiolus that was twice the height of the urn. I formed a column with the remaining four gladioli by placing two each side of the tallest, keeping them all upright. They were all positioned close together and each was cut a little shorter than the last and secured slightly more forward.

The lime was positioned to form a wide sweep which went from high and outward on the left-hand side to low on the right and well out over the edge of the container. All the stems radiated from the centre. The three fatshedera leaves were placed near the centre of the arrangement with a small one just in front of the first gladiolus, another small one horizontally over the left front edge, and the third and largest was placed in shorter between these two and faced sideways.

The rest of the arrangement was filled in with alchemilla but care was taken not to bring this too far over on the left side as this would have spoilt the line achieved by the lime. I covered the netting with the alchemilla and brought some of the lime through the centre. Variation of stem length is still important with this type of arrangement. The netting at the back of the container was also covered with alchemilla and the urn topped up to the rim with water.

Candlecup arrangement on a candlestick

This is adapted from the basic all-round arrangement and it makes a pretty centrepiece for a dinner table. I attached a candlecup to a glass candlestick and fitted it with wire netting. After tying the netting into the candlecup, I tied the candlecup itself to the candlestick with silver wire thus making everything secure. An extra large hole was left in the centre of the wire netting to take the candle. If preferred a well-soaked round of Oasis, cut horizontally to give a thinner disc, could be used instead of the wire netting.

I chose a white candle to fit in with my colour scheme of yellow, white and green and the plant material was yellow freesias, green hellebores, cream Cheerfulness narcissi, white heathers, widow irises, *Hermodactylus tuberosus*, tree ivy seedheads and tradescantia foliage. Trailing foliage is advantageous in this type of arrangement as it connects the arrangement with the candlestick.

My seven outline points were two hellebores, two Cheerfulness, one freesia and two heathers. I then filled in between these and introduced one of the three widow irises. The candle gave the height in the centre and flowers of differing lengths were arranged near the base of this. This arrangement was much flatter than the basic all-round one. I then covered the netting with foliage and found the heather particularly helpful in this respect. The two remaining widow irises were placed so that one was near the edge on the opposite side to the first and the other nearer the centre of the arrangement. I was careful not to place them in a straight line.

The groups of flowers were connected by placing the larger flowers short into the arrangement and leaving the smaller flowers with longer stems. The candle, however, stood well above the flowers and this is particularly important if you want to light the candle in such an arrangement. The ivy trailed low over the edge of the candlecup so that this was hidden. All the stems radiated from the candle. The arrangement was finished by covering the netting and topping the candlecup up to the rim with water.

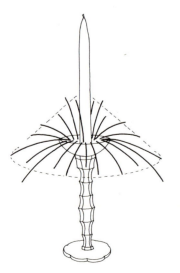

Arrangement for a modern setting

For this arrangement, which is very suitable for a modern setting and quick to do, I chose a bamboo container and three spider or Singapore orchids which echoed its style. I kept the arrangement very simple and used just five bergenia leaves at the base to cover the netting and to break the line of the container. Other flowers and leaves could easily be substituted. For example if you are unable to obtain large leaves, a few sprays of a clean cut rather solid foliage would do equally well. The bamboo container was fitted with a second inner container to prevent the bamboo from coming into contact with water which would cause it to split. This lining was made from a plastic washing-up-liquid container.

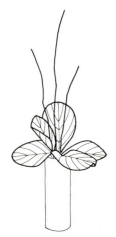

The three orchids were placed in first. The largest was three-quarters of the way back in the centre with the top curving gently away from the centre. The second, shorter-stemmed orchid was placed to the left side of the first and a little further forward in the netting. The third stem, shorter and more forward still, was positioned to the other side of the tallest flower. Flowers removed from the bottom of the orchid stems were used in helping to cover the wire netting.

The five leaves were placed around the base of the flowers to cover the netting and add weight. The tallest went at the centre back with the leaf at the left edge longer than that to the right. The middle two leaves were turned slightly to the side.

Cornucopia of marguerites

The cornucopia is the horn of plenty and an arrangement done in one must enhance its shape. Often these containers are fashioned in basketwork when they look lovely holding an arrangement of autumn berries and leaves. Mine, however, is made from white china and I decided to do a simple off-centre arrangement of marguerites. The white of the flowers picked up the white of the china and their clear yellow centres added an air of freshness. The only leaves used were very small ones of *Hosta undulata* which are variegated with a creamy white. I purposely chose a clear cut leaf to keep the clean lines of the arrangement. It was not necessary to use a pinholder or Oasis as the container is deep but I clipped the netting over the edge of the container to hold it in place.

The tallest flower was placed a little in from the edge on the more upright side (left) of the cornucopia and three-quarters of the way back. The length of this stem was between one-and-a-half times and twice the height of the container. I chose a reasonably small flower for this one but decided against a bud as I required a more definite colour at the top. A second, slightly larger flower, about a head shorter, went to the right of this. A third flower, again a head shorter, was placed on the other side of the tallest marguerite.

For the widest flower on the right-hand side, I used a bud which was showing colour. This flower was placed so that it flowed well out and over the edge. On the left-hand side I used another bud with a stem about half the length of the one on the right-hand side,

so that it too came horizontally over the edge of the cornucopia. The longest flower at the front edge was in line with the tallest at the back. All the flowers around the edge had curved stems so that they gracefully joined arrangement and container.

I then filled in the outline, turning some of the flowers sideways and forming a broken line. It is especially important to turn some of the flowers sideways when using those with flat faces as it prevents the arrangement from looking too set and gives it a more natural look. Some of the leaves were positioned next before bringing the marguerites through the arrangement starting from the widest points and working towards the centre. I placed the flowers evenly throughout, keeping the buds and the smaller flowers higher and having plenty of variation in length.

I finished by checking that the netting was covered, especially at the back, and topped the container up to the rim with water.

Pewter tankard

This is an adaption of the off-centre facing arrangement and I have included it to show you the shape which would be most suitable for a jug or tankard with a handle. With this type of container the height should always be fixed near the handle so that the arrangement flows down to the opposite side to emphasise the natural pouring movement. As tankards and jugs are deep, it is not necessary to use a pinholder or Oasis under the netting which can be attached to the handle to hold it firmly in place.

I used pink flowers with grey foliage—a colour scheme to complement the pewter. There were three pink hyacinths, seven pink arums (*Zantedeschia rehmanii*), three pink carnations, five pink Attraction tulips, three arum leaves, eucalyptus, *Senecio greyii* foliage, and lichen-covered branches.

The outline points at the top of the arrangement were marked with three pieces of lichen of differing lengths. The longest was in the centre with a shorter piece either side. A curved piece of lichen was placed horizontally on the right side of the arrangement. I then secured the main outline flowers in position using a tulip as the longest at the top flanked on either side by another tulip and an arum lily. For the width on the right-hand side I used an arum lily and on the left a tulip and I took care not to obscure the handle by placing this short-stemmed flower behind it. For the longest flower over the edge at the front I placed an arum lily in line with the tallest flower at the back of the arrangement. The outline was finished by placing carnations and arum lilies high on the left to low on the right with tulips going the opposite way.

The three hyacinths were the main centre flowers. One was placed towards the back, another over the edge at the front and the third to the side between these two. The three arum leaves were positioned quite close to the centre but care was taken not to place them in a straight line. One went on the edge at the right, the second higher on the left side and the third low into the centre.

Foliage was used to fill in and this was brought over the edge of the container and through to cover the netting. I arranged the eucalyptus with the arums and carnations and the senecio with the tulips. The handle was left reasonably free.

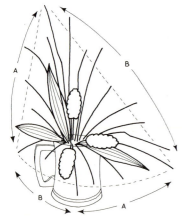

Top Cornucopia of marguerites
Bottom Pewter tankard

I finished as usual by connecting the groups of flowers through the centre so that they were evenly spread throughout with plenty of variation in stem length. All the stems radiated from the longest at the back. Finally, I made sure all the netting was covered and that the tankard was topped up with water.

Line arrangement of tiger lilies and grapes

This line arrangement was created on a rectangular green plate positioned so that the longest side was facing the front. I placed a small water-holding container on the plate and this held a large pinholder. Very few flowers were used, just three stems of exotic-looking orange tiger lilies. To add extra richness to the composition I included a bunch of grapes. Fruit can look very attractive when used in arrangements for a dinner table or for a cheese and wine party. However, the fruit chosen must blend in well with the flowers, either being the same colour or an attractive contrast. My choice here was green grapes to go with the orange flowers. There were also three pointed flag iris leaves to give interest and lightness at the top of the arrangement and five oval bergenia leaves.

The water-holding container was placed centrally, well back on the dish. It is always better to arrange fruit first so the grapes were placed slightly left of the centre and secured by means of a hook made from florists' wire which was twisted on to the stem of the grapes and then attached to the pinholder.

The three flag iris leaves established the tallest point at the back. These were graduated down to the left. One tiger lily went high to the right of the tallest flag iris leaf with the second low on the right to balance the bunch of grapes. The third and largest lily went midway between these two and slightly to the left. The pollen on the stamens of tiger lilies may stain the petals. To avoid this the stamens can be carefully removed from the flowers but it is more natural to leave them on.

The five bergenia leaves were placed as follows: a small one towards the back beneath the tallest lily; a second small one low to the left of the grapes; another slightly shorter than the second lifting up towards the centre; the largest low, to the right of centre and turned sideways; and the fifth lower behind the centre one and to the right of the first. The bergenia and flag iris leaves gave this arrangement clean cut lines and they lent a refreshing look to complement the exotic mood created by the grapes and lilies.

The leaves borne on the flowering stems of tiger lilies can make interesting additions to such an arrangement. I had to cut one of the lily stems short which left a piece of stem well clothed in leaves. I disguised the cut end by trimming it at an angle so that it could not be seen and placed these leaves under the front flower. The arrangement was finished by checking that the pinholder and container were covered and that the container was filled up with water. Other fruits can be used in flower arranging and they will create great interest. They add different colours, shapes and textures to compositions. Ornamental gourds, too, are excellent for unusual arrangements.

74   **Line arrangement of tiger lilies and grapes**

Arrangement in a piece of driftwood

Driftwood can be used as an accessory to an arrangement or it can become part of the container itself. I was lucky enough to find this particular piece of driftwood by a loch in Scotland and a small water-holding container can be wedged into position so that flowers and foliage can be arranged in the wood itself. The wood has been left in its natural state which is a greyish colour. The flowers I chose were all mauve—five stems of pointed liatris and five round dahlias with their buds. Five pieces of mauve ruellia and three pieces of mauve zebrina provided the foliage with three hosta leaves to give a clean cut effect in the centre.

A pinholder was placed in the water-holding container which was wedged in the piece of driftwood. The container was three-quarters filled with water. The height was established with three of the liatris. As usual each was a different length with the longest in the middle. The dahlias were positioned next, beginning in the centre below the liatris with a fairly small flower. This had a shorter stem than the third liatris. The second dahlia went well over the edge on the left with another shorter and higher behind it. The largest and shortest went in near the centre and the fifth dahlia was placed between this centre one and the tallest but to the right of both. I made sure that the flowers did not completely conceal the upright piece of wood to the immediate right of the arrangement.

The three large leaves were positioned so that one went towards the back and slightly to the right, the second went over the edge at the front to the left of the centre and the third and largest was placed slightly sideways between these two to the right. The ruellia trailed over the right edge at the front and higher to the left side at the back with the zebrina the opposite way. Some of each kind of foliage was used to cover the pinholder in the centre.

The last two stems of liatris were placed upright on the centre left, each being a different length with the second and shorter stem coming a little more forward in the container. I arranged the dahlia buds through the dahlia group. The whole arrangement was fairly upright so that the driftwood could be well seen. It was finished by filling the container to the rim with water.

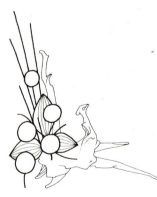

All-round arrangement in a brass bowl on a stem

This all-round arrangement was designed for a table centre so I made it lower than the basic all-round arrangement described in Section Two. The container is a brass bowl and I used yellow and green flowers and the seedheads of hypericum and nicandra. The bowl was fitted with wire netting and a medium-sized pinholder. I chose nine stems of golden rod, three stems of double spray chrysanthemums, three stems of single spray chrysanthemums, nine yellow dahlias, eleven stems of nicotiana, five stems of nicandra and five stems of hypericum. The individual flowers from the sprays of chrysanthemums were pruned and used on

their own. The foliage was made up from three pieces of skimmia, seven pieces of golden privet, three pieces of variegated rue, three bergenia leaves and three pieces of philadelphus.

First, the seven outline flowers—two golden rod, two double chrysanthemums, one nicotiana, a single chrysanthemum and a dahlia—were placed in position. The tallest flower in the centre was a piece of golden rod of about eight inches in height. Various flowers were arranged around this centre one including single and double chrysanthemums, dahlias and nicotiana. I then returned to the edge and placed flowers between the main outline points with stems of varying lengths. The nicotiana and dahlias were grouped together and the golden rod was brought through between the single and double chrysanthemums.

Arrangement in a piece of driftwood

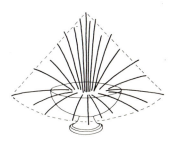

I filled in with foliage and introduced the seedheads of hypericum and nicandra. The golden privet and rue were grouped with the double chrysanthemums; the nicandra and philadelphus with the dahlias and nicotiana; the skimmia with the golden rod and the bergenia with the single chrysanthemums. Finally the various groups were connected, building up to the tallest flower at the top so that the finished arrangement was fairly pointed.

Dolphin arrangement

The container used in this arrangement is fashioned in the shape of a dolphin holding a shell with his tail. I decided on an off-centre facing arrangement with the height on the right-hand side. I determined the side of the height by following the line of the dolphin's tail through and this is a good rule to follow when arranging flowers in either a dolphin or fish container. The arrangement was comparatively low and spreading because of the shape of the shell. The shell was fitted with wire netting and a pin-holder on the right-hand side where the tallest stems were secured.

The flowers were as follows: one bunch of pointed white acidanthera; three stems of yellow and white alstroemeria from which I removed some of the side flowers to make the stems lighter; five stems of small cream dahlias; three stems of the yellow spray chrysanthemum Yellow Marble, again pruned to make them lighter; three large yellow dahlias for the centre, and seven white asters. For the foliage I used three sprays of abutilon, some sprays of snowberry (symphoricarpos), three variegated rue seedheads, five stems of honeysuckle berries, five variegated sprays of geranium, three ivy sprays and three hosta leaves for the centre.

A stem of acidanthera was used to determine the height, with the flower curving slightly to the right. To either side of this tallest stem I placed a pruned-down piece of alstroemeria and a second acidanthera. The width on the left-hand side was marked with a curved stem of acidanthera which projected well out over the edge of the container. The widest point on the right-hand side was established with a shorter pruned piece of alstroemeria. The longest flower over the front edge was an individual flower from a spray chrysanthemum.

The flowers grouped from high on the left to low on the right were alstroemerias, asters and dahlias together with the berries of honeysuckle and abutilon and the seedheads of rue. The other opposite grouping was comprised of acidanthera, spray chrysanthemums, snowberries, variegated geranium and ivy.

Once the outline was in position, I placed in the three yellow dahlias. These did not go too high in the arrangement as they were large flowers. One went towards the back, the second over the edge and the largest slightly to the right of the tallest. The three hosta leaves were placed to frame these dahlias. The back and front ones faced each other with the centre one turned slightly sideways.

The netting was covered with foliage and the flower groups were connected through the centre. Some of the snowberries were left fairly long on the left-hand side to balance the curved-stemmed abutilon on the other side.

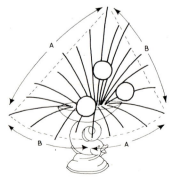

78

Index

Figures in italics indicate an illustration.
(Where an arrangement is referred to, only the page on
which the description starts is indexed together with either
its black and white or colour illustration. Every arrangement
has one or more line drawings.)